AUTHOR TONY GILES was born on the west coast of England young age with Cone Dystrop and Photophobia, an extreme sensitivity to light, he maintained some vision until the age of eighteen when he lost all sight except for his ability to recognise bright sunlight. At the age of six, he developed nerve sensory hearing loss that has progressively worsened over time.

Despite this, Tony gained a Bachelors of Arts Degree in American Studies from Northampton University in 2001 and a Masters Degree in Transatlantic Studies from Birmingham University in 2003. He has travelled from a young age and continues to enjoy experiencing new parts of the world, his most recent journeys including trips to the USA, Sri Lanka and Iceland.

Seeing The World My Way is Tony Giles' first book. He is currently working on its sequel. When he's not travelling, he lives in Teignmouth, Devon.

Published in paperback by SilverWood Books 2010
www.silverwoodbooks.co.uk

Read about Tony Giles at www.tonythetraveller.com

Text copyright © Aileen Milsom 2010
Maps copyright © Jenny Scott 2010

ISBN 978-1-906236-38-0

British Library Cataloguing in Publication Data
A CIP catalogue record for this book is available from the British Library

Set in 11.5pt Sabon by SilverWood Books
Printed in England on paper from sustainable sources

Seeing The World My Way

A totally blind and partially deaf guy's global adventures

Tony Giles

SilverWood

*Travelling is like sex
– if you think about it too much, you never do it!*

Tony Giles

Acknowledgements

My deepest thanks go to my family who have supported me throughout my entire journey. Special thanks go to my wonderful mum, Aileen Milsom, for having the foresight to send me to a specialist boarding school, which provided me with a normal upbringing. I'm forever indebted to you for having courage and strength, for having such zest for life and strong determination to fight my every cause, no matter what the odds or the obstacles. Your attitude has instilled in me those same qualities, without which I could not have considered travelling alone, or indeed undertaken such extreme adventures. I will never be able to thank you enough for helping with all my research, map reading, planning, photocopying documents, and arranging many other items essential to my travels, particularly ensuring I always had the necessary medication. Knowing that I was safe and happy, your only concern for me has made my travels and life an enormous success. Thank you, Mum.

To my sister, Annette Giles, thank you for being a huge help to me in writing this book, not only with research and spellings, but also for constant encouragement when I felt it would never be completed.

My thanks go to Carol Johnstone, the mother of a friend I met in Washington DC, United States on one of my later trips, for her sterling efforts and many long hours spent both in proofreading and in coordination. Without her extensive and tireless work, this book would not be complete.

Similar thanks go to Celia Morris, a volunteer from a local blind organisation in Birmingham, and her mum Eunice Woodhead.

I'm indebted to all my educational institutions for helping to improve my life, and for providing me with the confidence and skills to travel independently.

Thanks go to my disabled school friend of long standing, Will Harris. You introduced me to the fun of hostelling; we have enjoyed many journeys together, both at home and abroad. The fact that you can only see in one eye and often go round in circles, usually with me linked to your arm, has provided many hilarious adventures, just too numerous to mention.

I have to thank the staff in the American Studies Department at what is now Northampton University. Your willingness to help tackle any problems I brought with me was most commendable; my acceptance onto the American Studies course enabled my travel and study in the US, thus establishing a platform for my later journeys.

Geoff Parsons in South Carolina was magnificent in organising my study support in the US, which allowed me to travel once there.

Had it not been for the University in Northampton and my opportunity to study in the US, I would not have met such amazing people as James Gardner (Jimmy G) and Will Clarke, who became good friends. You did more than put up with my erratic, often rude, uncontrollable behaviour, many drunken episodes and occasional verbal assaults.

Likewise, I would not have met Kate O'Brien or Marcia Paul, had I not been able to study abroad. Both ladies have remained good friends and have grown to be as close as family. Kate is one of the few lucky (or maybe unlucky) people to have travelled with me and helped to make my journeys become considerably more exciting and fun. A young, sexy lady – I could not get enough of your friendship, with your charming, irrepressible personality – you gave me a reason to travel to Australia. Marcia is a wonderful lady, with patience and an amazing gentle personality. You taught me so much about life. You provided a warm, understanding friendship and a place to stay whenever I needed one; you are truly remarkable. My thanks to you both.

I owe many thanks to the Student Travel Association, for their diligence, time and effort in helping with my many travel requests and searches. To the numerous transport staff I have met around the world, for their help and patience in guiding me through stations, airports and on to further destinations successfully. To the many hostel staff for making my visits as easy and as comfortable as possible. They arranged activities, guided me to shops and pubs, helped me around the accommodation and extended their hospitality, often beyond their prescribed duties. I'm indebted to them all, as together they helped to make my travels a happy experience.

Thanks must also go to Mark Cooper from Manchester Action for the Blind, for your support with helpful suggestions and contacts for publishing.

Several people have provided support with spelling, grammar and general information, these include Gareth Thomas, Nick Freear and Nicola Berry-Salgado, friends I have made through my studies.

I must thank my publisher Helen Hart at Silverwood Books, Bristol, England, for editing this work and putting it into print.

Finally, my thanks go to all my fellow travellers, both named and unnamed, in this work. Without you, I would have no story to tell.

Tony Giles
Devon 2010
www.tonythetraveller.com

To my loving father
J. Derek Giles
who sadly passed away on 1st August 1995

The man who helped me begin my many journeys

Author's Note

Currencies mentioned in this book are approximations only and subject to change. I have noted the currency of the country involved, giving its exchange rate to the British pound during the time of my visit. I have used US dollars when British pounds were unavailable.

Various measurements are used throughout this work:

Length

1 inch	=	2.51 centimetres
1 foot	=	30 centimetres
1 yard	=	91 centimetres
3 ft 4 ins	=	1 metre
1 mile	=	1.760 yards / 1.6 kilometres

Weight

2.2 pounds	=	1 kilogram
14 pounds	=	1 stone / 6.8 kilograms

Speed of travel

1 mile/hour   = 1.6 kilometres/hour

Temperature

Take any Celsius temperature, multiply by 1.8 and add 32 to get Fahrenheit. Do the opposite to convert to Celsius. Five basic examples for illustration:

0 Celsius	=	32 Fahrenheit
5 Celsius	=	41 Fahrenheit
10 Celsius	=	50 Fahrenheit
15 Celsius	=	59 Fahrenheit
20 Celsius	=	68 Fahrenheit

Prologue

This book is for all those travellers on the road having good times and bad times, laughing or struggling over the last hurdle with their backpack, friend and enemy, simultaneously. It is also for my family and close friends whom I have continually abandoned to go wandering, leaving them with the worry and distress of not knowing my whereabouts or whether I'm alive or dead. Without them I would be nobody, and I couldn't undertake my crazy journeys.

Finally, this work is for the many people who want to travel and don't know how. It is for parents who have problems understanding why their children want to travel, disabled or not. Maybe in truth it is a book for people who are just unsure of themselves and don't quite know how or where to find answers.

This book says if you want it, and have a heart for it, anything can be achieved. I desired it so badly that I travelled around the world solo twice. And if I can do it, so can you. I'm not the first person to undertake this and I probably will not be the last.

This is a unique story of madness, adventure, booze, drugs, sex and excitement, with the occasional travel story included for good measure. I hope my readers enjoy it; I certainly enjoyed the experiences!

Chapter 1

The Background

It happened when I was a child. I was about nine or ten years old, when my aging dad told me stories about his life at sea and on land. Unrealised then, he raised awareness in the unconsciousness of my mind, which touched a nerve and conveyed a sense of adventure and excitement, which awakened my already vivid imagination and planted a seed that blossomed years later. Although my dad tried to protect me he was, indirectly, largely responsible for my travel exploits. He was born in the late 1920s and went to sea just before the end of World War II (WWII). He joined the Merchant Navy as a wireless operator and continued to serve after the war. His career took him around the world, to Australia, Canada, and India. He told me stories about sailing up the St. Lawrence River into Canada where large and terrifying icebergs passed close to the ship's sides. He crossed Australia by train, from the east to the west coast, going across the Nullabor Plain – a journey I still long to take.

Probably embellished a little, my father's stories captivated my idea of travel, and provided a sense of adventure. Far away from home for long periods, he and his shipmates battled ferocious, dangerous seas on cold, dark nights. His adventures encouraged me to overcome any problems I would encounter during my solo travels. My father was a kind man with adventure in his heart.

My travel adventures really began when I was a teenager, when my best mate Will Harris, who has sight in only one eye and an incapacitated hand, introduced me to hostelling. I was nineteen years old, full of enthusiasm, energy and foul language. We were off to Norwich of all places! It's like going to the corner of the earth and back, a distant, seemingly unimportant agricultural and cold city. We went there for a rock gig, something I had been doing for a couple of years by then, so with our backpacks in tow, we set off for chilly Norwich. After a long train journey, we checked in at our previously booked hostel. We asked the owner to leave the door unlatched, as we would be returning late. The gig was far from the centre at the university, near the airport, but we eventually found it and enjoyed the show. Then things began to go awry, when Will suggested walking back. It was a crazy idea in the dark and in an unknown city, but I just followed, swearing profusely.

We eventually arrived back at the hostel and after entering easily enough, we went to our dormitory, but the lock wouldn't open. We tried both our keys, but it wouldn't budge. It was 1 am so we crashed in another empty, unlocked dorm. In the morning, the owner forced the lock, we collected our gear and left. What an introduction to youth hostelling and travelling! Nevertheless, I have continued hostelling ever since. Incidentally, I should mention I'm totally blind and eighty percent deaf in both ears!

That experience opened the door to a new and exciting world and I never looked back. I would not use any other accommodation, as hostels are in interesting locations and generally inexpensive. There is always a mixed crowd and it's a great way to meet new and fascinating people from all backgrounds. Hostels are ideal for any traveller and the Youth Hostel Association-Hostel International (YHA-HI) and other independent hostels are located in many countries, including the developing world.

I began by using YHA-HI abroad, but eventually found that they can have a stale atmosphere. I felt there were too many rules, such as no alcohol on the premises, smoking bans and curfews. The independent ones are usually much better in that regard, though they can vary alarmingly. That doesn't worry me too much, as I'm usually only after a bed and I can't see the mess! However, I still use YHA accommodation when there is no alternative.

I ventured abroad early in life, to the Greek Island of Rhodes with my parents when I was aged fourteen. I enjoyed sweating from the blazing heat, swimming in the Aegean Sea, feeling the dusty streets through my feet and eating as much spaghetti as permitted. I went on a school holiday to the US as a fifteen year old, and at aged twenty, just before I began university, a friend and I backpacked around the US for two weeks.

In that same year, I also visited Trier, a small southern German town, on an organised holiday. My first trip to South Carolina on the east coast of America for part of my studies was my first independent journey and what an experience it was.

These early travels helped me tackle such obstacles as busy airports, locating accommodation, finding where to obtain travel information and what materials to research.

The desire to travel came from my parents, and I acquired the skills to undertake such adventures from confidence gained while attending a specialist boarding school for visually impaired children that was far from home. I became independent early on and it precipitated my global explorations. The boarding school I attended had become an establishment for children with all disabilities. This was a bonus for me, as being surrounded by people with a variety of impairments was a tremendous education, which demonstrated to me that even though people are different they are still intelligent and have feelings.

My then best friend was suffering from muscular dystrophy, a muscle wasting disease, and was slowly dying. It had a significant impact on me, as his death at the age of just sixteen left a void in my life and I eventually turned towards drink as a refuge. I later found his death and the impact of his life on mine to be one of the greatest learning experiences. I often meet strangers journeying solo when travelling, have a couple of drinks with them, maybe do an activity together, and then we go our separate ways. My friend's death taught me to cope with these short relationships and their often swift conclusion.

My education continued with university, where I chose an American Studies degree as this would allow me to travel, gain an education and enjoy the fruits of life – mainly drink, drugs, and sex! I began drinking when

I was eighteen. I would probably have started earlier had it not been for boarding school restrictions. I drank because it's the English custom, and I felt it helped my recovery from depression after the loss of my best friend and my dad the previous year. I needed something to ease my mind and cider seemed to help. I started decently enough, but later I became exceedingly inebriated and was excluded from bars, including my local pub where I was given a six-month ban!

Having explored geography to an extent and history more thoroughly, I've been able to gain an understanding of the larger world. The combination of love and encouragement from my family and my former specialised education has enabled my overall general world knowledge to expand, allowing me to travel with relative ease later in life.

Chapter 2

The Question Why?

I have visited many places, experienced much through travelling, and have met different and marvellous people from varied backgrounds and nations. However, I'm still asked the question – why?

"Why travel, Tony?"

"What pleasure do you get if you can't see?"

These are good questions from a sighted person's perspective, along with many other queries. I go travelling for a plethora of reasons; some are trivial, and some are absolutely necessary. Each trip is undertaken for a different purpose: a new country to visit, and another challenge. The question that is asked by the sighted person to the non-sighted is meant on one level, but the answer has several responses. The sighted person just wants to know why a blind individual would desire to travel to 'see' another country. The immediate response to that question is "Why not?" The other answers are that travelling is more than just seeing the beautiful scenery or landscape with your eyes. It concerns using all the body's senses, being able to engage with people, feeling different textures of land and plants, eating unknown foods and hearing new kinds of music, being exposed to an alternative, exciting culture and emerging into another country's qualities, and to return home knowing more than I did before I left.

I journey in a unique way and obtain a slightly different world perspective. Like other travellers though, it is about the solitary challenge of pursuing an idea, imagined or otherwise, living daily on the bare necessities with sometimes little food and/or money. I wanted to find answers to questions and returned a little older and wiser, without my answers and with more questions.

This book also highlights how I travel: quickly, often desperately, like a hunted animal seeking a refuge. For many people, travelling on a bus for forty hours would be exhausting and crazy, but I find it part of the experience. My ultimate pleasure is actually moving, pushing the mind and body to its limits, asking the questions and gaining the responses. I often overdid it and I found myself saying, "No, enough", when I realized my goal had been accomplished. Every day is an exciting journey and a challenge for me. My desires motivated me each morning, with the anticipation of meeting new people or discovering greater emotions than those of the previous day, and constantly finding new experiences and learning about life and myself; that's the ultimate reason for all of these journeys.

For many people, their main aim in life is to seek employment, buy a house, and start a family – mine is to travel. Though I love my family and close friends, they were unable to help me find my true self. I had to escape around the world to do that.

I have the attitude and determination, and with the

right knowledge, and help occasionally, I can achieve anything. A close friend who has no money and is in unsatisfactory employment said to me once, "It's lovely for you, that you can pack a bag and disappear around the world for a few months." That is the ultimate freedom to me. I love that challenge of having the ability to go from A to B successfully, with only occasional assistance.

My friends are correct when they say I often have help, I'm guided to places, have food brought to me and am shown huge generosity wherever I travel. However, I put myself in that position and my personality and the kindness of others does everything else. I challenged my fears and overcame many of them; I discovered others and pushed every boundary possible.

Many components build a successful trip and the fewer problems there are, the better the experience. It should be noted that no matter how much planning you do, problems arise on every journey; in my case, this usually occurred from a combination of tiredness and drunkenness. It often happens because you are in the wrong place or because of problems with the unexpected climate or habitat. It is all part of the experience, so you cope with the situation or return home.

I have undertaken two large trips when I visited several foreign countries, and needed the correct currency for each of those nations. I'm often asked how I deal with money. I usually reply by saying I give it to women and they spend it! Seriously, I carry cash in a money belt and keep my credit cards separate. When using cash machines, another backpacker or a hostel staff member accompanies me. If there's nobody available, then I visit a bank in person and get assistance from a staff member. Nothing is foolproof, but I have only had my card stolen once; I was in England and was able to cancel it immediately.

With regard to cash, British notes are different sizes. I frequently use US dollars and have to count the money, as the notes are indistinguishable. However, notes from a US cash machine are invariably $20 notes. If I then enter a retail store and purchase an item that is say, $15, I know I should receive a single $5 note or five $1s in change. The $5 bill could be switched for $1, but it is unlikely to happen because there are usually too many people around. I'm more likely to be short-changed or cheated by taxi drivers or hostel managers, especially when negotiating key deposits.

The other question I can hear the reader asking is, "How do you feed yourself?"

I say, "Excellently thank you!"

Purchasing, cooking and eating food are my biggest travel problems; and my strategy depends on the country in question. If the food is inexpensive, as in South East Asia, then I usually indulge and eat out. When journeying by bus in North America then the usual delights are McDonalds or early morning breakfast diners, the latter I particularly like. After trying the different cultural foods, I buy simple products such as rice and cold meat, tinned fish or beans. Occasionally, I ask other backpackers for help with this. I plan as I go, consult my finances and ask directions to the nearest bars and food outlets. However, after three months of travelling, I get completely disinterested in eating and it becomes a chore. I still have no idea why this happens; perhaps it is due to the pace that

I travel or maybe it is the result of a repetitive diet. If anyone reading this knows the answer, then perhaps you could advise me for my next long journey...!

I maintain contact with home by email; I learnt to touch type at school before getting a computer with speech software. Fellow travellers read my emails for me and work the commands, and then I dazzle them with my talent, leaving many a backpacker amazed and intimidated by my typing speed.

Travellers and backpackers come from varying backgrounds. Students often travel after college or in between universities. A couple of girls or a trio of guys might go on a round the world drinking spree, mainly visiting Australia, New Zealand and the like. Most people do it once, find it tough and scary, but an unforgettable experience. My travel strategy was different, as my education enabled me to visit the US.

However, once I had been let loose in a foreign country, there was no stopping me.

Chapter 3

The American Conquest

Early Trips

Many people, including my close friends and family, believe I developed a love for the US while taking American Studies at university. It would be more accurate to say I feel a love-hate emotion for that large and diverse country.

My fascination began as a teenager. I grew up enjoying American TV programmes such as *The A-Team* and *Dukes of Hazard*, and I loved the action and noise. However, it was reading books that further developed this fascination. *A Cambodian Odyssey* (Ngor, Haing Dr, 1988) is the autobiography of a Cambodian doctor who survived a bloody regime. He lost his entire family in the process and eventually escaped to Thailand and then America. Later, I read *The Crucible* (Miller, Arthur, 1953) a play about the 1692 Boston witchcraft trials. I was given the opportunity to visit America with my school at the impressionable age of sixteen. My parents paid for me to cross the Atlantic to Boston, Massachusetts, on the upper eastern seaboard, for a week's holiday. By then, I was discussing geography and history with my step-dad and learning about life and the world.

Boston

My initial arrival in the States was exciting, although negotiating customs was scary. I stayed in what seemed a large and quite grand hotel with huge double beds in every room. I ate enormous breakfasts and was introduced to the US dollar.

Boston is arguably the birthplace of the American War of Independence, the 'American Revolution' (1776–1783). The Boston Tea Party, one of several preludes to the war, occurred in the city's harbour. I heard all about Bunker Hill and many other fascinating places, events and historical and cultural stories. My Boston trip occurred during the 1994-1995 Baseball strike, and despite the famous Red Sox being out of action, we still went to view the stadium and all of Boston's other famous attractions. I touched a white Cadillac and also had my balls crushed on a street fire hydrant, contraptions which are often placed in the middle of sidewalks. I also had my first steak, which was huge and delicious.

Inevitably, after reading about the witchcraft trials, we visited Salem, a Boston suburban town, where we heard a play about the historical event and were taken around the graveyard where all the hanged victims were buried. I discovered that American dates of birth and death are written differently to British ones, with the number of the month appearing before the day – one of the many signs of American separation from Britain. It was the British monarchy who created 'taxation without representation', one of the disputes that initiated the war that led to eventual American independence.

I returned to England feeling pro-American and

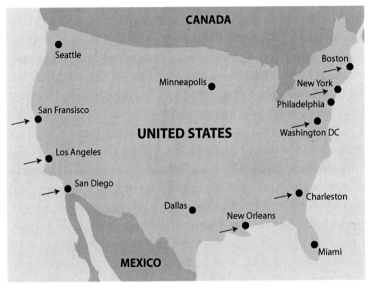

Fig 1: Map of the USA showing places I visited

ecstatic from my experience, due to the size and scale of everything and what I had taken to be friendly, talkative, positive people and a liberal opportunistic country.

Three years later, I returned to that so-called land of great promise and adventure with my disabled mate, Will Harris, to enjoy some backpacking before I began university. Will and I travelled with one eye between us!

Washington
We decided to spend a week in both Washington DC and New York City. I booked the hostels and the flights, including an internal flight from New York City to Washington DC, which in fact became my favourite place.

When we arrived in Washington, we took a taxi to the

Hostel International (HI), an expensive but wise choice. Washington DC Dulles Airport is difficult to get to or from at any time, day or night, and as we were in a new and reputedly dangerous country late in the evening, we felt a taxi was the safest option. The hostels in both cities were huge, with basements and small breakfast cafes. We met several people, including a Dutch guy who helped us get tickets for a tour around the White House.

This was June 1998 and the US was still relatively easy to travel and explore, unlike the present climate. We visited the George Washington and Abraham Lincoln memorials, using the interconnecting bridge. We took a tour of the old headquarters of the Federal Bureau of Investigation (FBI), which finished with an impressive and, very loud, gun demonstration. That excursion is sadly no longer available.

We walked the expansive streets in the hot June sun, drank as much free Coke as we wished in the diners and bars, such as the Hard Rock Café, stuffed ourselves on steaks and burgers and explored the small, but magnificent city. My enjoyment emanated from the fact that for a capital city, it was so friendly, with people from all races, and the tourist attractions were so accessible. Washington's famous monuments, the Washington, Lincoln, Jefferson and Franklin D. Roosevelt memorials, and museums, such as the Smithsonian, and the city's main attraction, the White House, are all centred within a 9-mile (15 kilometre) radius. They are all within easy walking distance of each other, making sightseeing comfortable.

I was almost shot when I tried to move close to President Lincoln. I had stepped over the guard rail to get a closer inspection and feel the huge monument, when a security guard told me to stop what I was doing and turn around, but luckily he relaxed when he realised I was blind. Will and I also paid our respects to John F. Kennedy (JFK), at Arlington National Cemetery during one sweltering afternoon. We walked for what seemed like hours before finally discovering his tomb. He was one of America's more interesting presidents who was assassinated arguably for his political policies on 22nd November 1963 in Dallas, Texas.

We finished the Washington tour by crossing the Potomac River to visit General George Washington's historical and splendid Mount Vernon home. Will and I wandered around the farm grounds and explored the mid-eighteenth century house. We spent five days in Washington before heading to New York City, the 'Big Apple', for more sightseeing and my first 4th of July party.

New York
We took a swift 'elevator' up the Empire State Building so Will could admire the magnificent panoramic view, and briefly visited Grand Central Station, the city's main rail terminus. The station affected all my senses, the noise was deafening and the smell from the trains and the brightness from the dazzling lights were so overwhelming I felt nauseous. One of our best days was spent getting to, exploring and returning from New York City's outer islands. We went to visit the Statue of Liberty and climbed up as far as we were allowed, unable to go to the crown due to ongoing reconstruction. Alas, the statue can no longer

be completely climbed due to the threat of terrorism.

We also spent an interesting day getting to the Bronx, where a proportion of New York's Chinese population reside. Again, this nearly got me killed. We took the subway and as the train entered the station, Will noticed that we were in a carriage that was beyond the station platform, so we made a quick dash from our carriage to get to one that was in line with the platform in order to alight. While opening a door to reach the next carriage across the couplings, I slipped and trapped my leg between the two carriages. The train was on a bend and luckily Will managed to rescue me and help me get my footing before the train straightened, or my leg would have been crushed between the two coaches.

We visited the Bronx Zoo that housed the usual animals. There was a cable car and train that took visitors across the park. We were in town for the 4th of July bash, although we decided to watch it on TV rather than be crushed by the vociferous crowds on the streets who were embracing the celebration of capitalism. Coincidentally, it was also the city's birthday – one hundred years of modern day New York City – this had begun with the construction of Brooklyn Bridge some years earlier, which joined the islands and created one gigantic city still evident today.

I had some interesting experiences in New York, but decided I didn't like the city. My dislike stemmed from the extreme pace of life there, and the brashness of the people in a city that never sleeps. One morning, as Will and I bought tickets to catch an early subway train, we said "Good morning", and were told to 'fuck off'. Not what you would call a pleasantry, unless maybe you were in New York! Also, Will and I couldn't drink there because we were under twenty-one. This hindered our enjoyment of the city somewhat.

The best evening was spent at an Iron Maiden rock concert after Will had a chance sighting of information about the gig. We discovered where to get tickets, and decided it was an absolute 'must see' event. The gig happened in the Rose Bowl Hall in downtown Manhattan. It was a fantastic show as they played most of their hits. Unfortunately, I found myself in a fight when I accidentally head-butted a girl half way through a song, and was jumped on by several of her friends. I ended up at the bottom of a group, but did manage to extricate myself.

I found tranquillity in the gigantic Central Park. We searched unsuccessfully for a section named Strawberry Fields, which is a mosaic circle in memory of John Lennon, who was shot and killed in New York City on 8th December 1980. We found the large lake around which people jog in the early morning mist that blows in from the nearby Hudson River.

Will and I finished our trip with a day excursion to Philadelphia in the State of Pennsylvania, in search of the Liberty Bell. We took an early train through the Jersey tunnel into the State of New Jersey and on to Philadelphia on the Delaware River. The journey took us two hours and it cost $100 (£60) for a return ticket.

I sampled a Philadelphia steak and cheese sandwich, which was delicious, but very greasy. Will and I attempted to find the Liberty Bell; we did reach the river and the university that lay on the city outskirts, but alas, we never found the bell. After several hours walking, we decided to locate the Hard Rock Café and get a drink. This particular Café had Bob Dylan's very own motorbike behind the bar. It was reputed to be the one that had been involved in his 1966 accident that lead him into brief obscurity. Unfortunately, I was unable to touch it. It had been an excellent introduction to travelling abroad.

I discovered so much on my two American trips, both about the country's geography and politics. Although the first trip was organised and the second was with a friend, I established a system for handling currency. I counted my money and asked friends each day how much I had. I put the $1 and $5 bills at the front of my wallet and the larger denominations at the back. I learnt to memorise how much I had and the amounts I spent – organisation is the key. I discovered how to travel around a foreign, westernised country. I noticed that the pavements were expansive and the four cities I had visited were on a grid system. There was also a subway network that operated like the London Underground, though more difficult to understand!

I travel with a cane, and use the underground system by listening for the station announcements. I also count the stops in case no announcements are made. I use the public to assist me when changing trains and platforms. Finding an exit is easy, I have a choice of two directions and sweep with my cane until I find stairs or use my ears to listen for the noise of an escalator. Again, I use my hearing to listen for the sound of people to find entrances and exits. If in doubt, I stand still and look lost. This usually works, and I have people offering me help.

I had been introduced to hostelling in England and travelling in America was an extension of that, although communicating with people who thought and acted differently was a challenge. It was an educational experience, which helped when travelling in the US on later journeys.

Adventures in the South
I took an American Studies degree because I could not explore the type of British history I desired. It was a multi-disciplinary course comprising US history, culture, literature and politics from its European beginning to the present, and included a study exchange with a university in the States. My second choice university accepted me and I went to Northampton in the East Midlands, on a course that offered five months in South Carolina. I jumped at the opportunity and welcomed the challenge of travel, study and adventure in another country of which I already had some knowledge.

University was fun and studying in the States was tremendous. I left England in January 2000 on my first independent adventure abroad. My parents took me to the airport and said their goodbyes – the last time that has happened – making me promise to keep in touch, which I didn't. I flew to North Carolina's Charlotte Airport then took a one-hour internal flight to Myrtle Beach in sunny South Carolina.

On arrival, the Head of Overseas Students, Geoff Parsons, a knowledgeable gentleman in his early fifties, met me. He oozed southern hospitality, even though he originated from the north. Geoff took me for a quick beer, helped me to settle in and introduced me to the housemates that I would be sharing with for the four-month term at Coastal Carolina University (CC). I was informed of the rules, which included no drinking on campus, a problem I soon resolved. The University was dry – the South has strange rules, as the US drinking age is twenty-one. Ridiculous, especially as people are allowed to drive at the age of sixteen!

I settled in quickly, made friends with my tutors and explored the compact campus immediately... where I discovered that there were few sidewalks. A bit of a disadvantage for me, as I rely on them to navigate my way around. The South is largely rural and the majority of people drive, but I became mobile by following the grass edges. Many of the students came from the southern states, had their own cars and strange accents; there was a diversity of race and nationalities. One of my housemates was African-American and my nearest neighbours were all Canadian. We drank beer together, which we smuggled in constantly – they taught me how to shoot ball, by throwing a small basketball into a hoop attached to their living room wall. One of the guys would stand underneath the hoop and clap and I would lob the ball, learning to judge the distance. I eventually became quite good.

I asked fellow course students to read for me, enabling me to research and make friends simultaneously. A student in my Vietnam War class named Marcia, (who has subsequently become one of my closest friends), said that on entering class with my cane I appeared confident, to the point of arrogance; she said I was friendly and eager to make conversation with everyone.

Marcia and I met one afternoon to study and formed a loose friendship. At one point, I asked her age and she smiled and said, "How old do you think I am?" I said, "About twenty-two, mam." She laughed and replied, "Old enough to be your mother." We would meet in class or in the canteen. Marcia had more classes than me, as she was a first year English-history student. The American academic system is vastly different as they have many small assignments, which I didn't find intellectually challenging. I got four A's for my efforts and believe me, I didn't work that hard, as I spent nearly all of my time drinking.

Marcia discovered that I drank; I expect many students did and I usually entered class with bloodshot eyes and smelling of booze. The problem was that I had too much spare time. I spent it either walking around campus in the dry heat, or running between buildings avoiding the short, sharp showers that South Carolina often experiences between January and May. Marcia was a mature student who had an interesting life perspective, having worked for many years – she taught me much about American culture. Her accent is indescribable; a southern twang, but not the drawl that many of the locals appear to possess. She is a small woman, with long, strawberry blonde hair and resembles a hippy from the late 1960s. We enjoyed discussing music and history. I taught her different study methods whilst describing British culture; she read to me and explained the laws of life.

There were other overseas students at Coastal Carolina

University. Two guys from my university – Jimmy G. and Will Clarke, a rock hippy who introduced me to marijuana, plus three Australians including one named Kate. She was a wild girl who I met one afternoon while crossing the wooden bridge that divided the campus. She was a tall, long-haired blonde with a curvaceous figure and aggressive mannerisms. Kate and I went to a bar just off campus one warm evening and got to know each other, getting inebriated in the process. We danced to a Led Zeppelin song in the middle of the bar, to an amused and baffled audience. Afterwards we attempted to return to campus, walking drunkenly together, going through a building site and attempting, unsuccessfully, to climb over a fence. It was hilarious and I ended up leaving my cane hanging on the fence. Only when we were back at Kate's digs did I realise it was missing.

The following day my friends set out to try to find it, as I was struggling without my trusted friend – although I did have a spare one just in case of such events. Eventually, it was found hanging exactly where I had left it the night before. This was the beginning of a friendship with Kate that is still strong today.

I was learning about the US constantly – by listening to both movies and talking books. I also chatted with other people on and around campus. I met a host of different people from all parts of the US and it became very clear that America was many countries combined. South Carolina, and the south in general, are fascinating – they are vastly different from other regions.

South Carolina was highly active in the 1861–1865 Civil War between the Union of the North and the

Confederacy of the South. The cotton slave states produced a historical land mass of intrigue and influence that is still a current topic for debate. When I was in South Carolina, January–May 2000, one of the hot discussions was the placement of the Confederate flag, which was on the State Capitol Building in Columbia and was a relic of the Civil War and struggle over slavery. The argument produced much historical, cultural and racial debate from many quarters.

The State produces both cotton and sugar and traditionally had slaves who worked in its agricultural industry. The area has several beaches including Myrtle Beach, which is a tourist trap near CC University, and there are numerous golf courses. The beach area contains a plethora of bars, restaurants, fun rides and shops, paralleled by a beach of soft sand running for miles-kilometres along the Atlantic shore. I will always remember South Carolina for its hospitality, slow pace of life, incredible food and the people's drawl, not to mention its cacophony of sounds and smells. In Myrtle Beach, I sampled the various beers, but constantly being asked for ID became exasperating.

One night my Canadian friends took me to Hooters! This is a bar with provocatively dressed female staff. We ordered food and the waitress asked me if I could see or not. When I replied 'no' she became very friendly. I enquired about her measurements and received a very pleasant answer. We flirted; I felt her hands and said she was sexy! As we left the restaurant, she gave me a hug and I had a feel of her firm hooters!

The food in South Carolina was unusual. I learnt to

eat grits, a southern delicacy that is almost indescribable; it just has to be experienced. Grits is made from coarsely ground corn and is boiled or fried with a little butter and, if you're lucky, some bacon. It resembles grey sand and is almost tasteless, with a gritty texture. In the south, you can eat it with every meal; I did and now love it. Other dishes included dried biscuits and gravy, which is often drab; and squash, a sweet vegetable. There are many varieties of beans; black ones which are hot and salty, butter beans which are rich in flavour along with the more recognisable ones such as kidney, green and chilli. The chicken is amazing; it is cooked in every way imaginable including hot and spicy, fried, BBQ, and smoked, all over easy. The pork is plentiful. I had catfish, which is salty and caught in the local rivers. The majority of the food is sweet, and a favourite is pancakes with syrup, jam or jelly. Ice tea is the sweet Southern non-alcoholic beverage.

The other topic of interest is the local language and mannerisms. I learnt to say 'Sir' and 'Mam' to older people. Another phrase that is sometimes used in the South is 'son-of-a-bitch', which is a more colourful expression. I also heard the words 'y'all', which mean 'you all' and has several uses. People also used the word 'nigger' which surprised me, as it's so derogatory. I first heard it being used when I went into a bar one afternoon. A bartender said, "We don't serve niggers."

Welcome to South Carolina, I thought.

The word doesn't offend me because although I find racism unacceptable, I appreciate that it's part of US cultural history and people's attitudes are steeped in what they've grown up with. Change takes time.

My studies and drinking increased. I did extremely foolish things when I was drunk – even feeling Kate's breasts one night after having a few too many. I was a little crazy and Marcia worried about me. I was after the ultimate experience, the desire to discover and try everything. Even Geoff commented that I embraced life, and made the most of every experience.

During the Spring break, most of the foreign contingency visited Disney World in Florida. I organised an excursion to New Orleans in the southern State of Louisiana, on the banks of the Mississippi River. With Geoff's help, I bought an internal flight, booked a hostel and headed for the humidity and alligators of New Orleans, to explore the city, enjoy the jazz and blues, and visit the French Quarter. This was an amazing trip.

I only informed Mum about my excursion after I returned to CC University, but on hearing about my escapade, she was elated. I had visited somewhere on my own, and that was an achievement that established my independence.

Chapter 4

From New Orleans to California

New Orleans
My time in New Orleans was wild. A friend gave me a lift to the airport, and I took a taxi to the hostel. I had been told just to appear, as there would be plenty of room. That prediction could have been costly because I'd just missed Mardi Gras, the annual carnival, by a day and the city was still overrun with people. However, the hostel staff were really accommodating and found me a bed. I had a top bunk in a small dorm in the back. The hostel had a relaxed atmosphere, very quaint with an outdoor quadrant to sit and enjoy morning coffee and bagels.

The metal bed creaked constantly. There was no ladder and I had to climb into bed by pulling myself up from the bars at the end, which attached both bunks together – I found it easier to jump down to get out. I was usually drunk, so that didn't help the noise factor and also made toilet journeys arduous, but I ended up staying for six days.

On my first day I stored my small bag and struggled to make my bed, then went in search of a member of staff. I wanted directions to the city's most notorious place, Bourbon Street, second only to the French Quarter, which was also reputed to be worth visiting. After a brief discussion about where to go and where to avoid, I got my directions and was told that trams went to Bourbon. I asked for a map with the hostel marked on it to show people if I got lost. I walked out of the door and stood on the hostel steps.

And then it hit me – fear, as I had never experienced before.

I felt hot and sweaty all over my body. It must have been 35C (95F) with humidity in the mid nineties, but it wasn't the heat that terrified me. The idea of going alone, blind, to find an unknown landmark in an unfamiliar, dangerous city made me panic. I began to shake. My breathing became rapid. My leg muscles shuddered and I struggled to maintain my balance.

I took a deep breath and said to myself, this is what it is all about; this is the challenge you wanted; you have the ability, now get on with it or go home! So I turned left and walked up the street to find the tram stop.

I had a ball that first evening and all the nights to follow; it was an amazing experience. I remember little about the city, except that the music was exquisite, the food hot and tasty, and the beer excellent. With a little help, I found the tram stop and made it to Bourbon Street. When I alighted, a large black man with smooth skin helped me across the tracks and onto the sidewalk. I guessed he was black from the way he spoke. I first stopped outside a street bar that sold bottles of cheap beer where I bought two.

There were many music bars with their doors open and people mingling about; the street performers were trying to sell their talents to anyone who would listen. I soon discovered that the street was pedestrianised, making it quite safe to wander from each bar in any direction I chose. Navigating was easy, as I just counted the small roads I crossed, taking care to keep within the eight or so blocks that had been advised, as New Orleans is considered one of America's most violent cities; alongside Washington DC, Detroit and Memphis.

However, I had few problems since I stayed among pedestrians and spent most of my time in the bars. I had a delicious grilled steak in a small restaurant before wandering into various bars asking about their best beer and its price. With regard to finding a table and ordering food, I just entered and stood until a waiter or waitress noticed me and asked if I wanted to be seated. When they requested my order, I would enquire what meat was on the menu – this usually worked fine and most bar staff were hospitable. I eventually found an open garden bar with lighted tables. Entry was free and there was big band jazz. They played until around 2 am. Many of the clubs were free to enter and the diverse music was marvellous.

I did attempt to do some travel excursions, as one of the essays for my course in South Carolina was to be about my trip to this lively and exciting city. What I did learn was that Bourbon Street is where all the cultural, musical and social activity occurs and stretches for about sixteen blocks. The scene is very open-minded and everything happens there – all night drinking, strip shows, brothels, prostitution and live jazz and blues. I was told that naked women hang out of upstairs windows. It was a crazy area and there seemed to be a constant surge of electricity in the air.

I went in search of the Tourist Information Centre on one occasion, only to learn that it had relocated, and after reaching it, I found it was closed. Wandering back, I came across an old man who was extremely drunk, someone who attempted to give me a needle and some ladies of a sexual nature! I was only after a beer and a chance to escape the stupendously uncomfortable heat. This was my first experience of tropical weather. Myrtle Beach was warm, but New Orleans was suffocating. It is in close proximity to the Gulf of Mexico from where it acquires its tropical weather. The constant humidity was the real killer; I dripped sweat continuously.

Eventually, I found a small, secluded bar and went in for a drink. I discovered the reason it was so quiet, apart from the fact that it was only 5 pm, was that it was a gay bar. However, I was only after a drink; nobody hit upon me and the bartender was friendly. We talked and drank in harmonious content. He asked about England and I enquired about his city. I moved on and found some food and stronger beer; I tried some Cajun Gumbo, containing meat, spices and vegetables. I then went to a side street bar that sold beer for $1 a pint. I stayed there until closing time, which was about 4 am. After that you would think I would be ready to go to bed, but no, not me. I was returning to the hostel in a taxi when I asked the driver if I could get food anywhere at this hour.

He replied, "This is America! You can get anything you want, brother!"

He dropped me at an all night diner where I had breakfast American style, three eggs sunny side up, four small sausages, bacon, a pancake, hash browns, biscuits in gravy and grits, of course. Then the real surprise! I got beer! Yes, at 4 am I was able to purchase alcohol! Bloody hell, I thought, why isn't England like this?

I took an alligator excursion, which included a city tour. At the river, I waited with others to board a long, narrow boat, which was to take us down part of the Mississippi to find alligators and have explained to us how they were caught. We filed onto the boat and sat in rows on wooden benches. The captain and crew were all Cajun, ancestors of indigenous people from Nova Scotia (formerly Acadie). These people fished and lived on the river and hunted for alligators on the shore and in the swamps. There was a strong, foul smell, produced by the humidity that came from the Gulf of Mexico and the Mississippi River. It tickled the nose and throat and added to the heaviness of the atmosphere. We were informed that alligators are reptiles that are smaller and weigh less than a crocodile; they grow to about 12–15 ft (4–5 metres) in length, usually sleep all day and eat sparingly. We did eventually see some alligators lying on the river bank further downstream, in the shade of over-hanging trees, asleep in the day's heat; it must have been 33C (low 90F) and only mid morning.

Several alligators were spotted in the water, which excited many of the passengers. The majority of my fellow-travellers were noisy, careless, ignorant Americans who were occasionally quite rude. I asked my neighbour to describe the alligators and he said they looked like tree logs, which is the usual description when they are in the water. One came very close to the boat. A small snake was passed around, which I was able to touch. Snakes are not as I imagined, they are far from being slimy and they rely on body senses to survive in the wild.

While we watched the alligators, it was explained how the Cajuns would shoot at their brains with a rifle after enticing them with meat on a long pole. We passed by small homesteads and learnt that the whole captured alligator would be used for meat and the bones for jewellery. On returning to shore, I tried some alligator meat cooked Cajun style, extremely hot and spicy. The alligator tail burger was so hot that I thought it was on fire; it tasted like chicken and was quite chewy.

My last night in the city coincided with St. Patrick's Day, which was a hoot, as the Irish-Americans say. The drinking began early and finished late. I managed to wake early enough the next morning to get a strong cup of coffee before catching my return flight to Myrtle Beach. One of the last things that I remember was drinking my coffee that last morning, sitting outside in the midst of a thunder storm with the rain pounding down and it being unbearably hot and humid. It was an amazing experience.

Back in South Carolina normality returned. I smuggled in beer, took night-time wanders, missed lessons etc. I did have to work harder in the second part of the term as I gained another subject and thus increased my study hours. Nevertheless, this still didn't deter me from having fun.

One night Jimmy G. and Will introduced me to marijuana. The three of us plus Kate took a walk around the campus, and we ended up on the large wooden bridge. We stopped half way along and passed a joint round. I eventually had a smoke, while Will explained the process. It was tricky, as I had to learn by touch, but eventually I figured it out and the inhalation hit the back of my throat and tickled my lungs; it was tremendous and I felt somewhat higher. It produced a laugh or two, and tears – I passed the joint on.

Marcia and I continued to build a friendship; she told me about shag clubs, people who shagged on the beach and how some girls have fanny bags. I got really excited – only to be informed, sadly, that a shag in the South is a dance, and a fanny means your bum not a woman's vagina. Another word that deserves explanation is 'fag', which means a cigarette in the UK, but in the US means a homosexual. I taught Marcia what bugger meant and what a bog was. She did become concerned about my drinking, especially when I failed to appear for class two days in succession and could not be found on campus for four days in a row. When we did eventually meet up again, I just explained that I had been sick!

I learnt much during my time in America, noticing that the majority of people drive rather than walk; most TV programmes contain adverts; the TV media is ferocious and the average diet consists largely of meat and fat. I discovered that many Americans lacked the basic knowledge of their country and that some students were low in confidence, while others appeared arrogant. I left Coastal Carolina University and travelled for a month before returning to England to complete my education and plan new adventures.

However, before I turn to the trials and tribulations of California, I must reminisce about the night I broke a sink!

It was late April and nearing the end of term. It was

Jimmy G's birthday, and a group of us went to town to celebrate before the dreaded exams. We bought a couple of pitchers, large jugs containing four or five pints of beer, and shared them around. I tucked into the beer as if it was my birthday, not Jimmy's. We visited a liquor store where I bought a bottle of Teachers Scotch whisky. We headed back to Jimmy G's dorm, breaking every campus rule. I was put on the sofa, given a shot glass and left to enjoy my whisky, while Jimmy G. and the gang made Bloody Marys and other concoctions. The beer flowed and I kept refilling my glass, before discarding it to drink from the bottle. It was good straight whisky, the way it should be drunk; no water or ice as the Americans make it. I talked little when I drank, only uttered the occasional comment or curse.

After I had consumed about a third of the bottle, I began wandering about the flat, apparently talking in a drunken stupor. I remember nothing from this point onwards. I walked back and forth between the sink and the toilet, passing the bedroom where the gang were holed up smoking joints. Everyone was pretty drunk and getting stoned. They laughed at my antics. Apparently I began swearing loudly, calling Kate names and saying I was going to kill her. Eventually, I quietened down and was forgotten. They must have thought I was so drunk that I had gone to sleep.

However, I had fallen against the sinks that were beside each other and collapsed to the floor and somehow rolled underneath the basins and onto the pipes. I was discovered around 3 am when Jimmy G. went to the toilet, and after washing his hands discovered that water was leaking through the floor into the lower flat. That was when he found me – unconscious. He and the others attempted to wake me. Jimmy G. and Will threw water over me and slapped me; eventually they got some movement and a confused grunt. I had managed to discard my watch and dislodge one of my hearing aids, which was on the floor, happily whistling to itself. Unfortunately, I had fallen onto one of my legs, it had become numb, and I was unable to walk.

They managed to get some degree of movement from me and with the help of the American boys from the house below, picked me up and carried me back to my dorm through some woods, to ensure no one was discovered. They got me back successfully and dumped me on my bed, put a bucket next to me to make sure I didn't choke on my vomit if I was sick, and then left. At that stage, I was still incoherent and knew nothing of what was happening.

Things were fine until I decided that I needed the toilet some time around 5 am, when I managed to get out of bed and into the corridor. Then my dead leg gave way and I fell, hitting the back of my head on the wall, causing a large bloody gash. Unfortunately, as I hit the floor swearing, I woke the remainder of the house. One of the guys who was entering the house late saw me; his name was Jason and he was the quadrant resident's Assistant; marvellous! I managed to return to the sanctuary of my bed, but then proceeded to vomit all over the wall and mess myself.

Terrific, what a performance!

Jason, assisted by Brian, another of my housemates,

attended to me then went in search of my friends. He woke them up, confiscated and destroyed their alcohol, and told them they should have taken care of me and not let me get into such a state. This was slightly patronising as they said, "Tony can look after himself."

Jimmy G., Will and Kate came over to rescue me. What a sight I was, drunk, smelling of whisky and vomit with a cut to my head, dripping blood and my pants full of shit. They bandaged my head and threw me in the shower, cleaned up my mess and put me back into bed. I slept for another forty-eight hours, remembering little when I woke, but felt particularly rough. I only heard the full extent of my escapade when I went to thank the guys for attending me. Boy, what a night! They were slightly annoyed that their booze had been confiscated, but generally thought it hilarious… Tony being Tony.

My last week at University was a quiet one. I passed my exams easily; bid Marcia a fond farewell and promised to stay in touch. She had heard about my drunken escapade from other sources, but she had been great. She had helped me a lot and looked after me as much as I would let anyone. I was a rebel without a cause, a loose cannon and just out for adventure and discovery.

What followed was all of that. I was California bound with Kate! We had become buddies, and since she was heading home that way, we decided to team up and see what mayhem we could cause on the west coast.

Los Angeles

I caught an early flight to Charlotte, North Carolina and then joined Kate on a long haul flight bound for

Los Angeles (LA), the 'City of Angels'. Kate and I were different people back then; I like history, she's not interested. I eat meat in large quantities, she's a vegetarian. This made dining together an interesting challenge. We landed in LA on a hot, smoggy afternoon at the beginning of May, and I had booked a flashy hostel in the Venice Beach area where we spent five nights. We took a taxi to the Backpackers', sharing the cost, as we did with almost everything. Kate became acquainted with a hostel receptionist named Brandon, a really short guy who only reached my chest. We met a young couple from Northamptonshire, England, where I began my University studies, which felt uncanny.

Venice Beach is classy, with expensive bars and cafes; it has a nice beach, but it was busy with eccentric American tourists. We also took a hostel-organised trip to Hollywood Studios. My blindness allowed Kate and I to jump the queues for the rides. Kate thought that was fantastic and said I had my uses. I recall a pirate ship that descended rapidly; I felt the sudden drop send waves of electric energy through my body, which tingled my nerves. We also went on the Jaws ride, which drove us round in a big-wheeled amphibious bus. We went behind the scenes of several films, including Hitchcock's Psycho. Kate thought it was funny as everyone said I was Psycho. We even found a very apt t-shirt for me that had the word 'Psycho' and lots of blood on the front. I have a morbid sense of humour that surfaced frequently during my Californian trip.

On reflection, I was a bastard towards Kate; I often wound her up, took the piss, and called her names like 'little possum', but we got drunk together, laughed a lot and learnt much. Kate hadn't met many blind people before, so travelling with me gave her a different life perspective. She would get defensive whenever she caught someone staring at me strangely, but I just laughed at it. The fact that I was independent with a sense of humour and was reasonably intelligent provided Kate with a sense of understanding. I helped her gain self-respect and enhanced her confidence. She taught me to view people and situations differently, such as vegetarianism and femininity. I was used to just looking after myself, but now I had someone else to think about; it changed my travel outlook.

I found LA a disappointment; it was large, had dirty areas, was full of smog and very humid. However, we stayed in a clean neighbourhood with friendly people. Brandon, the receptionist, took us music shopping one day and invited us to his place. He left me there alone while they went and bought some booze. When they returned with the drink, we just chilled. Brandon and I discussed our mutual love of Black Sabbath, the Ozzy Osborne years. Kate liked the Beatles and Brandon had plenty of their music, a real Californian boy. We rocked and relaxed.

Brandon also took us for a ride in his truck, a 'ute', one night. I jumped into the open back, but was told this was illegal, so we all crammed into the cab, with Kate in the middle and me going crazy to the music on the radio. We drove down Hollywood Boulevard and passed through Beverley Hills. It was fantastic driving at midnight with the music on and Kate looking sexy beside us.

Kate and I visited a small bar on several nights, where we talked about life and love, got drunk on beer and mudslides, and listened to the smooth sound of jazz. A trio consisting of a female vocalist, a pianist, and a blind guy who played the harmonica, kept us entertained. A Mudslide is a delicious cocktail of vodka, coffee liqueur, Irish cream liqueur and ice, of course; they put ice in everything! We found an English bar near the hostel that offered fish and chips and served excellent cider. The hostel was large, had many beds and was very busy, and for $28 a night, it was expensive, but that is how you learn. It had all the usual facilities, plus friendly staff. Next door was a travel centre where we purchased our Greyhound bus passes. My blindness allowed Kate to accompany me for free as my guide.

San Francisco
It was a lovely evening as we entered San Francisco; Kate described the scene, the Golden Gate Bridge spanning the harbour, the fortress of Alcatraz standing formidable in the background and the bright orange sun setting in the backdrop, highlighting it spectacularly. I was excited and could not wait to explore the city and its history of rock and hippies, architectural treasures and around 140 hills to walk. We had scoured my Lonely Planet Guide for hostels before we set off and I booked one, near the bus station, having decided that the Fisherman's Wharf hostel was too expensive. We walked to the hostel, and found it quite easily after checking the Lonely Planet map. It was a small derelict place, in a poor neighbourhood. Kate said she saw many people lying or sitting on the streets;

one guy was picking food out of a McDonald's rubbish bin, which sickened her. I had read about such poverty in the American metropolis.

After absorbing the hostel's dirty conditions and somewhat unfriendly atmosphere, we decided to stay only one night and find other accommodation the following day. We were in separate dorms; I was met by an extremely hostile Portuguese traveller who was very uncomfortable about sharing with a blind person. I complained to the staff and moved to another dorm. Kate was really angry, but I just shrugged. The place was decrepit; the walls needed painting and there was no washbasin in the toilet opposite my dorm. Kate told me not to go up on the roof alone, as I would probably fall off the bloody thing and kill myself; I just laughed. She was nice like that, but I preferred to tease her rather than listen.

We discussed tactics and decided to move the next day. We found a cheaper hostel in Chinatown, on one of the many hills; it was much cleaner, though it was on the fifth floor of a big apartment block. It was tiny, but had friendly staff. We booked for five days, but this was extended. We visited different bars each night, mixed with people in the cramped hostel and learnt even more about life. On our second night in 'Frisco, two staff members, Stephan and Neil both from England, took us out with about twelve other backpackers, to explore the nightlife. We walked to the centre in search of entertainment. In an Irish bar, I was hit upon by the biggest and gayest guy you could ever meet – just my bloody luck! He met me coming back from the toilet after the second round of drinks and followed me back to the group. He was about

6ft 6in tall (over 2 metres) and was huge. Why he took a liking to me, God knows; I was probably asking for it, since 'Frisco is known for its heterodox society. In short, anything goes in San Francisco. We could not shake him off; he followed us to each bar we visited. Finally, the guys threatened to kick the shit out of him if he didn't beat it – he got the message – what a night! The music of that summer was the Red Hot Chilli Peppers with their Californication album. Every time I hear songs from that album now I remember being back in Frisco having fun with Kate.

We visited Alcatraz. I booked two return tickets for $15 each on the ferry across to the island penitentiary. The prison had held some of America's most notorious criminals, including the Bird Man, Machine Gun Kelly, and Al Capone. One gloomy morning, we took the ferry from Fisherman's Wharf across the treacherous, narrow channel to the island. We were provided with audio headphones that allowed us to listen to the history and tales of the penitentiary and explore at our leisure. While passing through the different sections, we were able to view the main cell complex where an attempted breakout had occurred. We passed cells used by Al Capone and Frank Lee Morris, who, along with two brothers John and Clarence Anglin, were the only men reputed to have escaped the prison walls. It is still unknown whether they actually escaped the island and reached the mainland, or were washed out to sea in the ferocious current.

The penitentiary was closed by Secretary General Robert Kennedy, brother of JFK in 1963 and has subsequently been used in several films, most notably, *Escape from Alcatraz*, directed by Clint Eastwood (1979). I would recommend this excursion to any adult. The place was cold, damp and eerie; I felt the coolness and moistness on my skin. The island was isolated from society and an ideal location for dangerous criminals. After spending about two hours there, we returned to the mainland and spent the afternoon in the bay area, enjoying the sun when it eventually arrived.

We had lunch in a café and this was where I made my first big mistake of the trip! I ordered spare ribs with barbeque sauce while Kate had a veggie dish. I picked the ribs up and ripped the meat off the bones with my teeth, spraying sauce all over my lips like dripping blood. It was only after several mouthfuls that I noticed that Kate had become much too quiet. I realised how my actions must have appeared to a vegetarian, unpleasant. I had ruined her appetite. I apologised profusely, but the damage had been done. I finished my meal, paid the bill and we went out to listen to a steel band while relaxing by the harbour.

Kate and I walked the Golden Gate Bridge one sunny, but wet lunchtime. We took a couple of buses to Golden Gate Park and walked the magnificent bridge. It was a strange walk; on one side of the bridge there was rain while on the other there was warm, if weak, sunshine. I felt the massive concrete pillars and Kate read about the bridge from a plaque on a wall.

The Golden Gate Bridge was the World's longest suspension bridge span when it opened on 27th May 1937. The bridge is 1.981 miles (2.737 km) in total length and connects San Francisco Peninsula with Marin County. Although an engineer named Josith Strauss takes the credit for the bridge's design, he was aided by architect Irvin Morros who gave the bridge its Orange glow and senior engineer Charles Alton Ellis who, along with Leon Moisseiff, were largely responsible for the final design and structure.

Although Kate and I were staying in Chinatown, I managed to try several other continental foods including Mexican and Japanese. Saki, the Japanese spirit was tasteful, but lacked a creative spark. Kate enjoyed San Francisco immensely and liked the hostel even more. We debated whether to stay or not and discussed several options. She wanted to stay, but I desired to continue travelling, eager to explore as much as possible while I had the chance; it was my traveller's instinct.

It was on this note of indecision that we left things, and went out on what I thought would be our last night in the city. I got hammered and shared a couple of strong joints with some of the boys. Thus, on arriving back at the hostel sometime in the early hours, I was met by Kate whose first words were, "I'm staying."

Not "Hi Tony, how are you? How was your evening?" just, "I'm staying."

Well, that pissed me off and since I was already pretty drunk, I said some harsh words and we upset each other. I became even more drunk and then tried to apologise. Consequently, I woke up late the following day, missed the early morning bus to San Diego and had to spend another day in Frisco. Kate and I made up, realising that we were different people at alternative points in our lives. I also felt I could do it alone. I had recognised a weakness when travelling with people; I depend on them more.

When there is someone else, particularly with sight, I let them do all the research and planning. I relax and begin to rely on that person much more. Someone has to ask the questions and when there are two people, one person usually does it all. I realised that when I travelled alone, I shared out this responsibility amongst different members of the public and hostel staff. Nevertheless, travelling with Kate was a tremendous experience, though it demonstrated to me that I preferred travelling by myself.

Journeying alone is great because you don't have to make any compromises or sacrifices. If you want to get drunk every night or have early starts each day, then you can. Nobody tells you what to do or how to behave. In truth, I don't like the responsibility and enjoy the freedom. Travelling independently affords me those luxuries.

San Francisco is definitely a city of hills, lots of very steep hills, as we discovered on our explorations. The downtown area is complete chaos, but then so is almost every large urban US city. We took a bus downtown on several occasions, but the weekends were murder. The buses went in one direction and cars went in another; we just went round in circles, and often had to take taxies. The city contains the unbalance of several immigrants begging on one corner, yet on the opposite one an expensive jewellery store, which defines the complete social and economic paradox which is the United States of America.

San Diego

I took a Greyhound bus to sunny San Diego, some twelve hours down the coast and arrived as evening was falling. It is the cheapest if not the most comfortable way to travel in the US. I was in the last American city before the Mexican border and Spanish culture. I briefly considered going, but decided that time was against me and settled for three lovely days in the enchanting city of San Diego.

This city hosts not one, but two Hard Rock Cafes, one of my favourite places to socialise. The city had clean, spacious walkways, fantastic, soft sandy beaches, Southern California's longest pier at 1,971 ft (676 metres), good, inexpensive music stores and people from every part of California, except possibly San Diego. I stayed at the excellent Ocean Beach hostel, the staff being mainly Australian and New Zealanders. I took a city bus tour that gave a commentary. It passed the main attractions such as the harbour, Sea Life Centre, and the world famous San Diego Zoo. People were able to alight and board the bus at leisure. It cost $20 but was a relaxing way to explore the pleasant city. I managed to have at least one steak and found some strong, sweet cider. I also heard a couple of local bands in a bar close to the hostel. I walked along the nearby beach each day and found a good record store, where I chatted about music with the friendly owners.

Hawaii

The state of Hawaii is an archipelago with eight main islands. It is situated in the central Pacific Ocean, approximately 2,387 miles (3,700 km.) south-west of San Francisco. It was the last and fiftieth state to join the Union in 1959, hence the 1970s TV programme called *Hawaii Five-0*. The islands were captured by the US during the early imperialistic adventures in the late

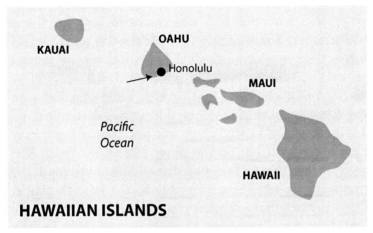

Fig 2: Hawaiian Islands visit

1890s and were a native Queendom. British sea captain James Cook was the first European to discover them in 1770 and named them the Sandwich Islands. Hawaii was a native kingdom from 1810 until 1893 when the monarchy was overthrown and became an independent republic until it was annexed by the US in 1898. The present population comprises of a vast mix of nationalities, race and cultures.

I returned to Los Angeles and caught a five-hour flight to Honolulu, the State capital, situated on Oahu Island. What a fascinating place to spend the last part of my audacious first independent adventure abroad.

My accommodation was a simple but spacious hostel in the countryside. It was a naturally built structure owned by a native Hawaiian lady. There was a small kitchen and a few dormitories. It was hot and humid. The main part of the hostel comprised a garden, pivoted by a huge palm tree that was the main base for flying cockroaches. These vermin actually flew! It was like JFK Airport for roaches, amazing! I was lucky none landed on me.

My main objective was to visit Pearl Harbor – an absolute must visit! I discovered buses serviced all island destinations and I could catch one just around the corner from the hostel, but on the other side of the road. The problem was that as I reached the middle of the road, the crosswalk changed direction due to the island's shape. Oahu is a peculiar island; it resembles a light bulb on its side. However, I managed to cross the road successfully and took the bus to the depot where I had to somehow find the connection to Pearl Harbor. I asked several people, including a couple of bus drivers, and managed to find the right bus. The friendly driver dropped me right outside the entrance to the memorial park. I was even more fortunate as while I was walking up the driveway to the National Park and shrine, I met a young American couple who had just moved to Hawaii; they asked me if I would like some help visiting the memorial. I said "yes" and thanked them. We entered the museum and went into the auditorium to hear a talk describing the events at Pearl Harbor. The following is a brief explanation of what occurred on Sunday 7th December 1941.

At approximately 8 am, Hawaiian time, the US Pacific Fleet naval base was attacked by Japanese torpedo carrying fighter-bombers. Several ships were disabled, the worst being the *Arizona* which was directly hit by a large bomb, causing catastrophic damage. 1,102 of the 1,177 sailors killed, lie entombed near the harbour entrance – at low tide the *Arizona* is still visible. Seven other battleships were damaged and some later destroyed. Much destruction was caused on land, in and around the harbour perimeter. There were many casualties, with 2,335 servicemen and 69 civilians killed and 1,178 wounded. Nevertheless, the main memorial is to the crew of the *Arizona*.

A small boat took us over the ship's tomb and onto a floating memorial where we were able to alight and visit the wall of remembrance. Many people laid flowers, as it was also US Memorial Day, Saturday 30th May. The air was very still and I felt a spiritual peacefulness surrounding the whole area. We had about ten minutes before we returned to shore, after which my new friends and I explored the ships that were on show.

Lack of time meant that I had a choice of seeing an old submarine or the notorious battleship, Missouri. I chose the battleship, never having been on one before. She was a massive craft, built in the mid 1940s for World War II and later was involved in two more conflicts. The Japanese official surrender ceremony took place on board the Missouri on 2nd September 1945, bringing an end to the war.

She was huge, with long sleek decks, large 16-inch (40 cm) guns that were used to pummel Korea's beaches and coastal towns in the 1950's conflict, and she was also used as support in the first Iraq War of the early 1990s.

As we walked through the ship, we passed through watertight doors, stepped over the large rims and climbed the many ladders to the upper bridge; I felt the scale of the massive vessel.

I spent my other two days on Oahu walking around Honolulu, visiting the beach and sitting in the Pacific Ocean, which was as warm as bath water. Unfortunately, I managed to knock over a set of surfboards while I was walking along the beach. They fell like dominoes, which was hilarious, especially as this guy came running up shouting, "No, no, go this way!" I just smiled and walked on!

I learnt about the volcanic mountain named Mauna Loa along with its other four volcanoes on Hawaii Island at a geological-historical museum, and discovered that it was the largest volcano on earth in terms of volume and area covered.

After four days of beautiful weather and nature, hospitable people and interesting walkabouts, I returned to LA. I was reacquainted with Brandon when I collected my large backpack from the hostel where Kate and I had stayed. I slept at the dump that is LA Airport for several hours, and then flew to North Carolina where I managed, with some charm, to catch an earlier flight than planned back to England. I took the train to Weston-super-Mare, arriving a day early and scared the hell out of my Mum.

When I rang the doorbell, she said, "What are you doing here?"

I replied, "I live here!"

She thought I was the postman. What a surprise!

I was back home at the end of a great life-learning adventure, one that made both my mum and myself proud of my achievement.

Chapter 5

Going Down Under

Reasons to escape

I finished my degree in the summer of 2001, dissatisfied with life and myself – I just wanted to travel. I longed to visit Vietnam, having just written a dissertation on a component of its wars. I was interested in the people, their culture and history, and I wanted to be there for Tet, the Vietnamese lunar New Year. If I could achieve that, then travelling elsewhere in the world would be a bonus. Tet was not until February 2002, but I could not procrastinate for six months, so I decided to visit Australia and New Zealand in the meantime.

I'd learnt about Australia from meeting Kate and other Aussies, and from listening to sport on the radio and TV – I understood how to navigate the country by its cricket grounds! I planned the trip through Student Travel Association (STA) and bought an all-inclusive round the world ticket.

Mum did much of the research and discovered the necessary inoculations required for South East Asia, and checked the climate conditions in various locations – I needed plenty of sun cream for Australia. I also required equipment such as a money belt, a waterproof shower bag, a small towel and a day bag that folded to the size of a tiny pillow (my US trips had taught me to travel light). I discovered that the Australian currency was $2.75 to the £1 during 2001–02. I photocopied all my documents, including a letter from my doctor that explained my sudden mysterious high blood pressure, and prepared for the big day.

I left for Australia via the US on 1st October 2001, just three weeks after the 9/11 US World Trade Centre attack, at a time when many people were dubious about flying and travelling in general. I had no such qualms; my attitude then, and now, is that if I'm blown up on a plane or it crashes, it is beyond my control. The only way to defeat terrorism is to continue living, which for me is travelling.

There was a six hour delay before I finally boarded the Trans-Pacific flight to Australia – first Sydney and eventually Melbourne. The LA airport staff were discourteous; people were very anxious after the terrorist attacks. I crossed the Pacific Ocean for the first time, but barely noticed, as I slept for most of the sixteen-hour flight!

Melbourne
When I arrived in Sydney it was raining heavily and I could have mistakenly believed I had returned to England after a thirty-hour journey. Airport Security checked shoes for incendiary devices, but I was excused from removing my footwear after my heels were checked. Once my passport and visa were examined, I caught my last flight and arrived in Melbourne around midday on

3rd October 2001, full of anticipation. I had booked a hostel called Melbourne Metro, the YHA near Queen Victoria Market in the north of the city. I took a bus into the centre and asked directions from there.

The hostel was big with many beds. I was greeted by friendly, but noisy, people who said "G'day" and "No worries, mate." I quickly adjusted to the language, and was told that an evening meal was available and that there was beer in the hostel dining room. After being shown to my dorm and given a bottom bunk, I changed from cold weather clothes to shorts and a t-shirt. I phoned Mum, tried to contact Kate, but she was unavailable. I asked directions to the city centre and was told the location of the nearest tram stop and given a map with the hostel highlighted. To achieve this, I had to first find a corner and then get to the middle of the large road adjacent to me.

One arrived moments after I located the stop with my cane. The driver rang the bell and said, "Hop aboard mate."

He seemed friendly, like the majority of Australians, relaxed and seemingly insouciant. I asked to go to the city centre and he dropped me near a main street, helped me off the tram and gave me directions. I eventually found myself in a crowded, commercial centre; people bumped into me and I heard heel shoes and smelt strong perfumes pass by.

Evening was approaching as I sensed the light dwindling. I briefly explored the area before leaving the main drag and searching for a bar. I was not worried about getting lost as I had my map and since Melbourne was on a grid system, I should eventually return to where I started. I found a secluded, underground bar. It was dark and quiet, smoky and hot. I ordered a pint of Victoria Bitter (VB). I was now in Oz, enjoying my first beer, savouring the cold liquid as it connected with my throat, slithering down my oesophagus, warming my belly. I had several pints and enjoyed the calm atmosphere, feeling immediately at home.

An hour later, I asked the bar girl for directions to the closest tram stop. I explained I was staying near Queen Victoria Market, luckily a notable city landmark. I found the stop and twenty minutes later, I was dropped near the hostel. I had to locate the actual building, which I did once I recognised the area, having walked a few blocks. There was an island in the road close to the hostel and once I had crossed that and located the nearby wall, I was back in familiar surroundings.

As I entered the hostel for the second time that day, my life changed significantly, as one of the staff asked me if I was Tony from England. When I replied, she said I had received an email from Mum with bad news. It said, 'Anthony, you have kidney damage, you need to see a doctor or go to hospital as soon as possible. You are very sick and you could die, love Mum.'

I was in such shock, I did what any adventurous youth would do – I went and got drunk.

The owner mentioned a hotel bar close by. Ten minutes later, after negotiating a road and a grass island, I found the hotel/bar. I discovered it was called Steve's Place and introduced myself to the barman and ordered a large VB. I got inebriated. The old bar was large, with a record player and a good selection of music. The next day I visited the nearby hospital.

I presented the email and necessary documents, and was taken to a day ward. General tests were undertaken and I answered some questions. My blood pressure was nearly 200 over 125, which is extreme under any circumstances. I had further examinations, urine and blood tests. I said I felt fine, had no discomfort and was travelling. I was forbidden any food, which was annoying. As I was a new patient at the hospital they had no medical history of me. Prior to leaving England I had been prescribed blood pressure tablets by my GP and was awaiting blood test results. There was a suspicion I had an under-active thyroid gland, but in time this proved false.

Eventually, a doctor appeared and said they wished to perform a kidney biopsy. I asked about the procedure and if it was necessary, and he said it was better now than later.

After discussing all possible risks, I agreed to the examination. I was taken to theatre where a female doctor, along with several delightful nurses, attended me. I was given a general anaesthetic just above the left kidney. The doctor hit my back about eight times and I breathed in and out when instructed, but I felt one hit traverse down my spine that terrified me. I have been through some events, but that was the scariest. The operation involved taking a slice of tissue from the kidney. The wound was sutured closed and I was wheeled to the ward to recover and sleep off the anaesthetic. I was told not to move for fear of breaking the stitches. The next morning I was discharged and asked to return in five days, and told to reduce my alcohol intake.

I returned to the hostel and found my belongings

altogether – nothing had been taken. I informed Mum of the medical situation and contacted Kate. We agreed to meet in the late afternoon. When she eventually arrived, we hugged and went into town to catch up. We had maintained a friendship via email and had become closer through that medium. Kate explained that she was banned from driving because she had wrapped her car around a lamppost while over the limit. I said, "You're as crazy as me!" When I told her that I had just spent twenty-four hours in hospital, she was surprised and somewhat alarmed. I said it was nothing much, not really understanding the extent of my kidney damage myself, and said they'd just told me to reduce my booze.

Kate invited me to meet her family. We took a short train journey to the south of the city. She rang her Mum on the way and Lawris agreed to collect us. Kate told me that you could be fined for swearing on the train. I queried this, but she was adamant. Lawris sounded more Australian than Kate, with a twangy accent. I met her Dad, Clive, and her brother Craig, who were both quiet. I explored the house and then we sat in the garden so that Kate could have a joint. She said her parents disapproved! Her family were lovely. I told Kate that I was in town for a week and we agreed to meet up one night after she finished work.

Clive drove me back to the hostel. I went to my bed, only to find someone else occupying it. I found the manager who showed me to another bed. I also discovered that someone had taken my flip-flops. It had been raining intermittently, so I had been wearing my boat shoes. My flip-flops had been under my bed. However, on closer inspection, I noticed that they hadn't been stolen, but exchanged for a leather pair. The only problem was that they had metal disks in the soles and were almost unwearable.

The reception had two sections, one for arrivals and departures and the other for excursion and travel enquiries. I went to the enquiries desk and chatted with the friendly female receptionist. She informed me about a city tour, which included visiting a wildlife park. They collected and dropped people at their accommodation. I asked about reserving a seat on the boat to Tasmania. Summer had just begun and although it was warm, it was not yet in the upper 30C (90F). This meant that the boat to Tasmania might have space. The girl booked me a seat on the boat leaving Friday evening, returning the following Tuesday, giving me three nights in Tasmania. The boat docked at Devonport, not Hobart. The return ticket cost just over $350 (£127), which included meals and entertainment. Finally, I asked about directions to the Yarra River and the Melbourne Cricket Ground (MCG).

I wanted to explore as much as possible during my five days in the city. I managed to find the Tourist Information Centre with help from several individuals who said "Over that way mate," and "No worries, have a good one mate." I asked about city walking tours, and completed a form so they could supply a volunteer assistant for me. I visited the old jail-house where, for $12, I received a one hour individually guided tour. I touched some iron chain shackles and visited the spot where Ned Kelly was hanged, which I found fascinating. The jail had housed men and women and was used during the

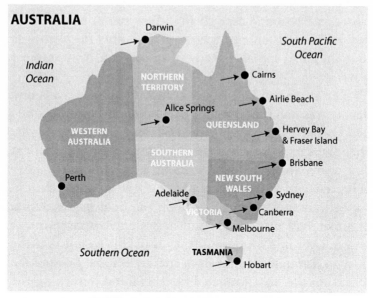

Fig:3 My tour of Australia and Tasmania

mid-late nineteenth century.

Later, I took the bus to the MCG complex. Unfortunately, I passed the stop and had to get another bus back. Once in the vicinity, I crossed over the highway via a large bridge, and on the other side, some kids showed me to the entrance along several paths. I finally entered the building, found the queue and enquired about the next tour around the sports museum and stadium. The ticket attendant asked me if I was with anyone. I said I was alone and had arrived independently. After asking if I could cope with steps, I was permitted on the tour.

The MCG holds Victoria State and International cricket matches. The arena has witnessed some famous test matches and players, for both Victoria and Australia, including Shane Warne, Steve and Mark Waugh, and the State's most successful batsman, Alan Border. The complex also hosts Aussie Rules Football; this is the unique national sport. It is a cross between rugby and Gaelic football, from where it takes its origin. There are nineteen players per team; an oval ball is used and there are several rules. The final occurred the day I arrived in the country. Australians are sport mad; they play and watch with equal passion. The MCG had held the 1956 Olympic Games, and there were measurements on a wall of the high jump and pole vault, and on the floor were the lengths of the world records for the long and triple jumps. We passed the Olympic pool, which had the names of all the famous Australian swimmers carved into the tiles.

When we finally ventured out onto the pitch, I walked on the grass of the MCG. The empty stadium felt vast. We sat in the east stand and the guide told us stories about famous moments that had occurred in the stadium. After the hour-long tour, I explored the Olympic Hall of Fame. I had a headphone set and pressed buttons near the exhibits of interest, which I found with some assistance. Just beyond the MCG is the Rod Laver tennis arena that holds the Australian Open in January of each year.

My day tour began with a cultural and historical introduction to Australia and Melbourne. We learnt some Aussie words such as 'chuck a lefty', 'chuck a righty' and 'chuck a uie' – which means 'go left', 'go right' and 'do a u-turn'! These were hilarious when said in the Aussie tongue! The guide even said something like, "Rip a skab off a beer and chuck a steak on the barbi!"

I loved the lingo.

We initially explored the city, where our guide pointed out the sights including the old jail. We entered the countryside, with a two-hour drive to the animal sanctuary. I got a feel for the land as we bumped along; there was highway with bush and eucalyptus trees, which the koalas like. Koalas are not the only species unique to Australia and Papua New Guinea: kangaroos, herbivorous marsupial of the macro pod 'big foot' species, Duck Billed Platypus, a semi-aquatic egg-laying mammal with a sensitive bill. Emus, crocodiles, deadly spiders, Black Widow and Red Back, snakes such as Viper, Cobra and Python, to name but a few. The land is still hostile once you leave the suburbs. The cities even have the possum, a pest that likes to eat through any wooden material it can get its claws or teeth into.

We had a brief tour of the park to see the different animals in their large enclosures. I felt metal statues of kangaroos and some stuffed koalas, platypus, black fox and a couple of birds. On the return journey, the guide explained about the countryside, and how the eucalyptus trees photosynthesise with little water but plenty of sunshine.

The weather was fine the next day, although by now I knew it could change rapidly. People say Melbourne can have 'four seasons in one day', and they are correct. I had experienced rain, sun and wind and the temperature had fluctuated frequently. However, on that day the sky was cloudless, I could tell by the increased temperature. It was at least 28C (86F). I walked to the Yarra River that divides the city North and South, and eventually found the bridge, after asking many people. However, to get a boat ride I had to cross to the other bank. I accessed the bridge without incident, but got into difficulty trying to cross it. First, I hit my head on a metal strut and then I became lost attempting to locate the information office. A man eventually helped me find the tour boats, and I paid for a one-hour journey. The excursion took me gently down river; a commentary described the buildings and attractions along the banks. I heard little of the commentary because of the engine noise, but I enjoyed the ride in the sun and developed my tan.

When the boat returned to its mooring, I went in search of food. A local guy helped me recross the bridge and showed me to a cafe. We chatted and he asked if he could join me, since he was on his lunch break. I agreed. I told him about my trip and he was suitably impressed. From his voice I discerned he was in his early twenties, he said he was employed in information technology. He was fascinated with my story. We swapped emails and mum also received one from him. He explained how we had met, and expressed his amazement at my endeavour.

After lunch, I went to the hospital where I had an appointment with a nephrologist. Again, my blood pressure was tested and more blood and urine taken. The doctor explained that I had severe kidney damage. He advised against travelling to Vietnam, but I told him it was the reason for my trip and that I was not going home for five months. He explained that if I contracted Hepatitis A, B or C in Vietnam, dialysis would be unavailable, and could result in my death. I said I could rearrange my itinerary and spend less time in Vietnam, but not avoid it altogether. The doctor asked me to see him in a week. Fortunately, I would be back from Tasmania by then.

Kate and I had agreed to rendezvous at the main train station. Being large, it was easy to find. However, locating Kate was harder in the crowd. Once she found me, we went and had dinner. Kate was in her work clothes and I guessed she must look fetching in a short skirt and tights. I told her about my escapades and she chatted about her work. After several drinks, Kate said she had to get home as she had an early start in the morning; she walked me to a tram stop and kissed me goodbye.

On my final day in Melbourne, around midday, I met a lady at the Tourist Information Centre and we took a three hour city walk. The guided tour was free. I told the lady I was travelling and was interested in history and culture. We inspected several rounded and oddly shaped memorials. One was for Australian bravery in the First World War, two others were for WWII, and finally we discovered the city's main war memorial. We ascended the steps and went in to listen to the bell of remembrance before going up onto the balcony. I was allowed to touch some old British cannons outside the army museum. I teased the guide about being Australian and she returned my banter.

After just one week, I'd really warmed to the land down under.

Tasmania
Melbourne's harbour, Port Phillip, is on the far south side, which I reached by taxi. A crew member helped me aboard the large ferry and exchanged my seat for a cabin, at no extra cost or fuss. I had to declare that I had no groceries or dairy produce, as Tasmania is very

strict about what and whom it lets in and out. Most of the habitat is natural bush and wildlife and they want to keep contamination to a minimum. My shoes were checked and I confirmed I hadn't visited any farms, rain forests or bush land.

I was shown to a cabin on the second deck of six. Immediately after leaving port, I headed to the first of the two bars on board. It was a night crossing which generally takes fourteen hours from Melbourne to Tasmania, across the Bass Strait, one of the world's roughest passages. I looked forward to this. I had heard about Tasmania from both the Sydney to Hobart yacht race and the cricket.

In Tasmania, I took a bus from Devonport to Hobart, the State capital, some eight hours away. The hostel in Hobart was attached to a pub. I had made a reservation while I was in Melbourne. Australia is great for backpacking: you tell the hostel staff your interests and destinations and they arrange the bookings. It is simple as many of the hostels are affiliated. Some staff even organise activities.

I entered the pub and asked someone directions to the hostel. They said next door, but it was full. I eventually found one of the hostel staff and said I had a reservation; he was a German guy of similar age to me. This simple place had two flights of stairs up to the dorms. I said they were manageable and asked him to just show me the way. The guy said food was available in the pub since the hostel was closed until 5 pm. I later booked a tour to Port Arthur, Australia's oldest prison, which I heard had a reputation for cruelty. The excursion also included visiting the Tasmanian Devils.

I was now in Australia's most southerly town. Hobart was an hour behind Melbourne and summer had just begun. It was colder there, with a chilly wind coming from the Southern Ocean (Antarctic). I left the hostel, turned left and kept walking until I reached the harbour. I followed the wind and the smell of the ocean. On the waterfront, I turned right and slowly walked along, sweeping with my cane for obstacles such as mooring bollards. I stopped frequently to listen to the sea and enjoy the sun's warmth on my face. Because of my light sensitivity, I noticed the fireball as it set in the sky, intensifying as it changed from orange to red and finally disappearing. I've never had colour vision, but could see changes in shade when young and remembered the different shades.

I eventually found a small bar that served food. I fought my way through the locals to the bar, found a stool, sat down and ordered a beer. I began chatting to some people almost immediately. The barman was friendly, very talkative with that lazy accent. Tasmanians have slower drawls, are relaxed and gentle, unlike some of the people on the mainland who are less friendly and lead more intense life-styles. I ordered some food and sat at an outside picnic table. A local couple, who were passing, saw me and came over to chat. We had a beer together and I gave the lady my salad. I had a delicious steak and then wandered back to the hostel, which I eventually found after getting slightly lost.

My Port Arthur trip was excellent; it was one of the best places I visited in Australia. I was collected just after 8.30 am, sleepy eyed; I had managed to arrive in the reception just as the bus was pulling in. We were going to visit an animal park to see the Tasmanian Devils being fed, and after an hour's drive through sparse bush, we arrived at the animal sanctuary.

There were two Tasmanian Devils in a large cage – a medium sized one and a small one. They were about the size of a small dog, black in colour, with fork-like clumps of whiskers on the top of their heads, hence their devil name. The keeper explained that the Tasmanian Devil is a carnivorous marsupial. They are nocturnal, have acute hearing and have the strongest bite of any living mammal.

They navigate and hunt by smell, as we were about to witness. The keeper tossed in a piece of meat, the Devils attacked it, the larger one smelt it first, grabbed it and began chewing. The smaller one smelt the meat and gave chase. They grunted and growled loudly. The small Devil managed to steel the meat from the larger one and ran off into a corner. For a few seconds the larger one could not smell it and all went quiet. Then the larger Devil found the smaller one with the meat and the chase re-commenced. It was a fascinating experience – I could smell their strong aroma and hear their loud grunts.

Resuming our journey, we were informed about Tasmania's habitat. The island is a triangular shield with Devonport at the centre of the North coast and Hobart in the southeast. The west and northeast coasts are lengthy with a shorter northern coast. The interior is mainly dense bush, with a large mountain in the centre. There are several trails coursing the island, but only 'bushwhackers', people who live in the bush and the natives, know about them. Apparently, there are no pure Tasmanian natives left; they had been decimated by contact with Europeans. All that remain are the offspring of inter-related marriages.

In the mid nineteenth century, Port Arthur became Australia's most notorious prison. A small timber station was built in the colony in 1830, followed by a huge flour-mill and granary in 1842. The first stone of the separate prison was laid in 1848. Our guided tour took us to the Major Governor's house, the cells and the infirmary where many prisoners went with physical injuries and viral sickness. The convicts, who were all in solitary confinement, were forbidden to communicate with one another. They were put to work shackled to a large stone in the intense heat for twelve hours a day, moving rocks and stones to build their own prison. The solid stonewalls of the cells were designed to destroy a man mentally, and many broke. Death in prison was common in the late eighteenth and early nineteenth centuries.

I entered one of the cells and felt the thickness of the walls and the iron bars. There were drawings on the walls, along with some faint writing. Each cell was 3 ft square (1 metre square) – dark and cold in winter and damned hot in summer. These were harsh measures for harsh times.

There was a chapel and a hospital and many convicts visited both. Few escaped, except two men who alleg-edly absconded in a wooden boat, getting as far as the Australian mainland before they were apprehended and returned to the prison – and undoubtedly executed as an example to others.

After the tour, there was time to buy a drink and/or

snack. Some people visited the memorial at the former 'Broad Arrow' café; one of the sights of the massacre that occurred on 28th April 1996, in which 35 people were murdered. We slowly returned to Hobart, stopping several times to view the Southern Ocean from a distance. The sun emerged briefly, creating a lovely sight as it diffracted on the water.

Back in Hobart, I returned to the harbour and had an exquisite local dish which I believe was Blue-eyed Trevalla, caught around Tasmania's shores. Later I took a taxi to an area containing several bars and clubs. It was dark by then, and raining hard, but the bars were still busy. I met five local guys; we swapped drinks and once the bar closed, they invited me back to their place for more beer and some hash. It was an upstairs house in a suburb. I accepted a bottle of beer from one guy. They were all in their early twenties. I told them about my trip, calling them 'mate' and saying 'no worries'. They were good-natured, which is characteristic of Tasmanians.

A water bong was passed around, which was a funnel that they showed me how to use. I covered a small hole at the bottom with my thumb and inhaled. The hash hit the back of my throat and I slowly got stoned. It was a relaxing sensation. A wave of energy went through me although I coughed slightly. After a few more drinks and laughs with the boys, I left.

I had arranged a guided walking tour for the Monday, and the German guy from the hostel took me to the tour office. The excursion should have cost me $50 but just as I was about to pay, three other people arrived which reduced the cost considerably. We had a walking tour of old Hobart, which I'd recommend to other travellers. We went through a cemetery where our guide, a local man in his early fifties, told a story about a haunting. We also went past the harbour and explored the city's back areas.

I had an hour-long boat ride around the harbour before returning to the hostel to prepare for my final night in town. I headed to the club I attended the previous night, although this time I arrived slightly earlier and it was much quieter to begin with. Whilst I was at the bar having a VB, a guy left $60 (£18) on the bar. He returned about forty minutes later and it was still there, untouched. Amazing – that would not happen in England!

I met a sexy Tasy girl who was wearing leather trousers, and we danced to the band and kissed. I also met an older guy who gave me a piece of marijuana as big as my thumbnail. I was unsure what to do with it, as I could not roll it. I stuck it in my pocket and ate it on the boat back to Melbourne. Needless to say, I don't remember much about the return journey!

Once back in Melbourne, I had my appointment with the Nephrologist who confirmed my kidney problems. He prescribed more blood pressure tablets and told me to get a monthly blood test. I purchased the prescribed medication and then had a lady in the Qantas travel office re-arrange my flight tickets and accommodation in Thailand. She then took me to a nearby hostel that had a travel desk in order to arrange a night bus to Adelaide. I also purchased a one way ticket from Adelaide to Alice Springs on the famous Ghan train, and asked the best way to travel down the east coast. It was suggested that I get an open Greyhound bus ticket for a month from

Cairns to Sydney.

That night I took the bus to Adelaide in the State of South Australia.

Adelaide

Once in the city after a restless night, I went to the hostel. The Backpackers was run by a lady in her late thirties who was surprised but impressed that a blind guy was travelling alone. I was given a ground floor dorm in a fairly large building, but it had no swimming pool. Further north, the hostels all seemed to have pools. There was little in the surrounding area besides a pub and a brothel; a larger bar/club was across the park.

Adelaide is a quiet city, named after one of England's lesser-known queens. It has a central square where the tram starts from and is surrounded by many old buildings. A park is lined with statues of bare chested women, as a symbol and reminder of breast cancer. Many German immigrants settled in this area. They'd come to South Australia with the help of a Scottish merchant who brought them to a new life and to escape from tyranny and persecution in exchange for cultivating the land. Through this system, places like the Barossa Valley were created.

There were several Irish people in the hostel who'd come to see their country play the Australians at Gaelic football, and so far the Irish were winning easily. One Irish guy took me to the pub through the park. This pub was the nearest place to get food and I had several pints of Cooper's beer. I had travelled west to Adelaide, reversed my watch by half an hour and changed my beer from VB to Coopers. The Aussie beer is good, but weak, and you rarely get pints. It is usually a small glass or a bottle with a foam Bebby, as it is called, to keep your drink cool. It gets so hot in the summer that a large beer goes warm quickly.

I went to the Barossa Valley with a small group on a wine tour. Our driver-guide explained some of Australia's history: the discovery of the land, Adelaide's name and about expeditions North into the wilderness, which eventually found water and later established places such as Alice Springs and Darwin. A fascinating story of bravery, disaster, determination and adventure in hostile conditions with wild natives, dangerous insects, reptiles and unbearable heat. I was following in those footsteps, but in a more comfortable manner.

We had a break after about an hours' drive into the countryside with coffee/tea and Vegemite rolls. Vegemite is similar to Marmite. It has a unique flavour and in my opinion tastes foul! We continued to the Barossa Valley to find our first vineyard. This area contains rich, fertile soil with a relatively good rainfall that helps the vines grow. I was not much of a wine connoisseur, preferring beer and spirits, but I was keen to try. The idea was to sample one wine, drink some water and try a different variety of wine. I preferred the white wine to the red. We spent about twenty minutes in each vineyard. We explored the region by bus, viewing the scenery of hills, valleys, vines and Eucalyptus trees; the fresh, hot, country air smelt marvellous. It was thrilling to be touring the countryside and I felt every shape of the landscape through the twists, turns and bumps of the bus.

We stopped for lunch at a large winery with a garden and picnic tables. I had a cheese and biscuit meal without the salad, and a couple of glasses of red, which tasted less bitter after food. There were more views and vineyards before the long, lazy drive back to Adelaide.

I spent one day at Glenelg Beach, reaching it by tram, although finding the stop was a challenge and I walked right passed it more than once. Glenelg is about an hour from Adelaide. On arrival, I asked the driver for directions to the beach as I was deposited at what sounded like a busy high street. To reach the beach, I had to pass through a hotel lobby then a car park before I arrived on the sand. I had a quick paddle in the sea and lay in the sun for half an hour before a strong wind sprang up. I had a delightful meal in a quiet pub before returning to Adelaide.

I spent the following day in more German settlements. I had the same guide as on my first trip and we joked together all day. I was with an older group this time, and the history I had heard on my previous trip was repeated, but told slightly differently. We visited two small fishing villages. I ate fish and chips with Kookaburra birds attempting to eat my food, and I felt a Blue Whale's tail, which was massive. In the afternoon, we visited an inland village where we stopped for tea and cakes. It was another relaxing day with more history and culture.

On my final morning, I had a quick tour of the Adelaide Oval cricket ground where test matches are played.

* * *

Alice Springs

I took the Ghan Train from Adelaide to Alice Springs, a slow, comfortable eighteen-hour journey that offered amusing Australian movies. The Ghan was originally a camel train that travelled between Adelaide and Stewart (later Alice Springs) in the late nineteenth and early twentieth centuries. The first steam train reached Alice Springs in 1929, which eased the journeys. Camels were introduced to Australia from North Africa. They stayed and eventually became a natural Australian species. The seats were comfortable and there was a bar, but I was disturbed hourly by a commentary stating that I was now passing some monument of significance. This even happened at midnight when I was informed that the train was passing the iron monument to Aborigines!

On arrival in Alice Springs, the hot, dry atmosphere greeted me as I alighted from the train. Alice is a small town and the hostel was close to the station. The area has since expanded and there are more hostels. I said I wished to stay for five days. The female receptionist was concerned about me getting lost around the hostel and falling into the unguarded pool, as the hostel was unstaffed after 8 pm. The complex was fenced, and could only be entered with a key and a code. She said she would have to ask her boss if I could stay, as she didn't want the responsibility for my safety. Her boss concurred, but suggested she contact a blind organisation to see what they could recommend.

Two ladies from the disability agency visited and we had a chat. I said I was travelling around the world independently. The dorms were on a raised wooden platform up some steps, away from the pool and had easy access. The ladies decided that if I stuck to this path and took care I should be safe. They told the hostel manageress that in their opinion I'd be no problem, so I settled in, got my bearings and the receptionist helped me organise some tours. I wanted to go to Ayers Rock, known to the Aborigines as Uluru. It was 280 miles (450 km) southwest from the town. The receptionist eventually found a tour company willing to take me.

I spent my first full day touring the city by bus, alighting and boarding at various places. My first stop was the camel farm. The bus collected me around 9 am and deposited me fifteen minutes later. We circled the town, and the driver announced the different stops. At the camel park, the driver helped me in and said he'd return in an hour. There was a large school group at the farm, so I waited patiently for my turn and requested a ride just as the kids were asked if anyone wanted a second go. The guy saw me then and took me through the fence. The camel knelt down and I asked her name – Alice, naturally! She was a large beast, but friendly, despite snorting. She wanted to join her mate who was in another field. Camels are amazing animals. They can carry enough water to cross half a desert, and their hump contains fat that provides plenty of energy for a long, hard walk in dry, sandy conditions. Their ears and eyes are adapted for protection against sand storms and they have coarse hair and rough skin.

Once in the saddle, I was told to lean right back while the camel rose, and I began my ride. Alice walked in a funny, jerky, unsteady motion and I was moved from side to side; it was difficult to stay on the saddle and very uncomfortable. I circled the paddock twice, holding on and leaning far back, and I slid off as Alice knelt down.

My next visit was to the snake farm. I touched several lizards and a gecko ran up and down my arm and across my shoulders. The keeper told us about a lizard that was cornered in the town square – apparently he found the first lamppost and shot straight up because lizards like to climb.

After handling several other lizards and seeing a couple of poisonous ones, we visited the snakes. These are beautiful, intelligent reptiles. They are not slimy, like many people imagine. This concept comes from snakes moving in a slithering motion. Most snakes tend to kill their prey by constriction, although many of the most poisonous snakes live in the Australian outback. There were two snakes together in a glass cage being fed, and the keeper said if the reptiles got too close when they were feeding, they would kill each other. He disappeared to find another of the keepers and when he was gone it nearly happened! The female and male were too close together and the keeper only just returned in time.

A black hooded python was produced. The snake was heavy and as thick as my wrist. I placed the python around my neck, where it explored and put its head in my armpit. Snakes like dark moist places; they mostly sleep all day because it is too hot in the desert, and appear at sunrise and dusk when the temperature is cool and moist. Our group of seven included a girl who was petrified of the snake. The keeper managed to persuade her to touch it briefly, but nothing more.

That evening I had a meal in a restaurant that offered crocodile, kangaroo, camel and emu on its menu. The four meat meal was delightful and only cost $22 (£8). Camel is delicious; it tastes like tender sirloin steak, the flavour of emu is similar to sweet chicken, crocodile is chewy and kangaroo resembles pork, but more salty.

An Irish girl and myself were collected from outside the hostel shortly after 6 am. A large man approached and asked aggressively if we were going to Ayers Rock, we both said 'yes'. He asked the Irish girl to look after me. He said I had to follow instructions at all times and that I could not, under any circumstances, climb the Rock because he couldn't take care of me. I retorted that I was independent, and I only needed guidance.

It was a long eighteen-hour day excursion. There were two driver-guides, and one drove each way. The terrain was dry desert with multi-coloured rocks, red, white, green, depending on where the sun shone on the different metals. The heat was intense with little shelter. This was real native territory.

Ayers Rock is a single sandstone boulder and the second largest monolith in the world. Ernest Giles was the first European to see it in 1872. The Aborigines had the area returned to them by the Australian government in 1980 and it opened as Uluru-Kata Tjuta National Park in 1986. Two out of three tribes object to it being climbed as they see it as their spiritual monument.

We drove at a cracking speed and arrived in the National Park around 12.30 pm. We were instructed to carry lots of water, wear a hat, have good footwear and use sun cream. Besides Ayers Rock there were several other rock piles, plus a canyon and a few creeks. Various park tours include a two-day trip where you are able to do a dawn or a sunset climb. We had the choice of climbing the boulder, weather permitting, or taking a two-hour walk around it.

I wasn't allowed to climb Ayers Rock because – as the guide put it – "I don't want to ask the Rangers to go up and break your fingers off to bring you down!"

We had a laugh together, and he relaxed with me once he realised I was quite capable.

The Irish girl went with an English girl to climb the boulder. Ayers Rock is a roundish shape, with different parts to the climb. There is a simple start before you get to a very steep section. Two thirds of the way up, an Irish guy who climbed it in the 1960s had apparently inserted a chain handrail to ease the situation, but it was only part way. Finally, to reach the top, you have to overcome an almost vertical gradient.

The first objects seen when approaching the boulder are the headstones for all the people who have died attempting to climb it – impressive, but a discouraging sight. The girls told me later that they climbed part of the way up, but looked at each other just before the arduous stretch and came back down. There are no handholds and it's sheer rock. It is a difficult climb and you could fall to a premature death at any moment.

I was able to touch the bottom of the boulder, which was hard and rough. We walked around in the dry dust and silence of the desert. There was no wind at all but when the older of the two guides helped me onto the first level of the boulder a strong wind arose. I was told that the bolder couldn't be climbed if the temperature was over 35C (95F), raining or very windy, and I could understand why. Climbing would have been arduous against that force of wind, regardless of the huge cracks that I found almost immediately stepping onto the rock. Some cracks were over 3 inches (7.5 cm) in diameter in places and over 1 ft (30 cm) in length. They were a dangerous obstacle for any individual.

We walked around slowly, exploring different parts of the park. There were indigenous carvings and more coloured rocks. One guy climbed the boulder and returned swiftly. We crossed a dry creek. I realized there was little water in the outback. I found it amazing being in that natural environment, which was so atmospheric. The vibes I felt were of intense energy that crackled in the air and on the hard, dry ground. The younger guide explained how the Aborigines lived. They were nomadic and camped in caves and near boulders. On cold nights, they slept surrounded by several dingoes for warmth. If tribes wanted to communicate, they had to leave a gift, like a stone, and put it in a circle drawn on the ground near another tribe's camp.

At 5 pm, we set up a barbeque and had some 'tucker'. The older guide said, "When the first shadow of the Rock begins, we go, because every other bloody vehicle will also be trying to leave."

Alice Springs is below the Tropic of Capricorn and in the southern hemisphere the light disappears rapidly at sunset. Once we saw the shadow of the bolder, we piled into the bus and headed back to Alice Springs after a fantastic day of history and knowledge.

We reached the hostel at midnight, stopping once on the drive back because one of the guides spotted a gecko on the side of the road. He got out, scooped it up and brought it aboard for us all to see. I touched it and felt the furry hood on the back of its neck. When a bird attacks, they grab this part, which then detaches and the bird flies away. The gecko is camouflaged against the desert floor and the driver only noticed it because of its shadow.

Another excursion took me into the desert to visit the MacDonnell Ranges. Our lady guide, in her late fifties, collected me and three other backpackers and drove into more of Australia's wilderness.

The MacDonnell Ranges are a 400 mile, 664 km series of mountain ranges. They consist of parallel ridges running east to west of Alice Springs. They were named after Sir Richard MacDonnell, Governor of South Australia when they were discovered by John McDouall Stuart's expedition in April 1860. In the twentieth century a farmer purchased a large section of the land for a significant amount of money.

The West Macdonnell Park was established in 1984 to protect the area. This facilitated the development of the Larapinta Trail, a world-class long distance bush walking trail that runs 139 miles (223 km) along the spine of the mountain range. There are notable attractions in this area including Ellery Creek Big Hole and Archers Pit amongst others. An hour's drive East of Alice Springs are sights important to local Arrernt people, many of which contain Aboriginal examples of rock art. These include Emily Gap, Jessie Gap, Trephina Gorge, and N'Dhala Gorge.

On the way to our destination we made the usual

breakfast stop at a roadside café. Our guide had a damaged right leg, and when she guided me, she wobbled. Apparently, she'd been in a serious car accident at the age of eighteen. She defied the doctors claim that she would never walk again and even walked down the aisle to get married just months after the accident. She had led a quiet life until her husband of some thirty years died and she was shattered. She said she spent a year mourning and then found the courage to travel to England by herself. She'd never been out of the country until then. After her experience abroad, she returned to Australia and began working as a tour guide in the outback. She drove the large, heavy van, camped in the bush under the stars and had formed a relationship with the tour company manager. It was a great story.

The Ranges were spectacular; they held a magical wonder and fascination. We were almost the only people out there. We visited three or four creeks with several vantage points and had a picnic lunch in one spot, attended by the usual Kookaburras. We continued further into the desert, but it was extremely hot, around 35C (95F) and there wasn't much shade. We had plenty of water, essential in the outback along with a hat, sun cream, a good radio, spare batteries and plenty of fuel. If you get lost or break down, there is only the air ambulance or air rescue to help. No traveller should contemplate walking alone because the Australian outback is one of the World's most hostile territories.

In the afternoon, we came upon yet another creek, and our guide told us it was one of the oldest creeks in the world, if not the oldest. It was just a small stream, similar to most other desert creeks, and full of pebbles. The guide and I walked down to the stream and I skimmed stones for a few blissful minutes. There was not a breath of wind and the whole area was silent except for our own footfalls on the terrain and the splash of stones in the water. As we retreated up the stones to the wooden platform that surrounded the small bar, the guide struggled on her wobbly legs and fell. I managed to catch her and we laughed about it. We had gained a mutual respect – she thought I was amazing to travel blind and unaided around the world, and I thought she was brave to live and work in the outback.

Our final stop was in an area surrounded by large rocks. This time we managed to catch a glimpse of some wildlife because high above our heads two rock wallabies were chasing each other. Wallabies are smaller members of the kangaroo family. Their grey colour provided camouflage against the rock as they chased, and the whole place echoed. As we explored, I was able to touch yet more rocks and the different colours stained my hands. Eventually we headed back to Alice Springs.

I next went to an Aboriginal reservation to listen to a cultural talk. The local Aborigine guides were in their early twenties, and explained how they lived, worked and hunted. They also discussed family values and their place within the cultural structure of Australia.

When I arrived, the group were throwing boomerangs. This weapon is a single piece of eucalyptus bark, shaped like a coat hanger, held in one hand at about shoulder height, with the flat part of the weapon away from the body. You flick your wrist powerfully to propel the boomerang and it's meant to kill a small animal and then bounce back to you. I also touched some other weapons that were used for fighting and hunting, including a long spear, a small round shield and a wooden club. Everything was made from the trees and plants that grew in the Aboriginal environment.

The weather in Alice Springs was extremely hot and I struggled acclimatising. I used the pool and jumped in naked one night after returning from the pub. I believed no one was around, so I stripped off and dived in. It was a small, shallow pool and I enjoyed the cool, refreshing water on my skin and splashed about for a time. However, as I was climbing out, I heard two people pass by. They must have seen my naked backside protruding in the air, but I didn't give a damn. I just grabbed my clothes and went to my dorm.

At the hostel I met an Israeli whose car had been stolen. He said the police were pleasant, but slow in finding the car. In the outback people are very friendly but lethargic because of the heat.

On my final morning, I had breakfast in the town centre where I waited for the bus north to Darwin. While I was eating I heard a couple of local entertainers playing the didgeridoo. This is a long, hollow, wooden Aboriginal instrument which is played by blowing across the top and down the didgeridoo. It makes a vibrating sound that when first heard sends shivers up your spine. Finally, with my two backpacks – one large and one small – I caught the Greyhound bus to Darwin, at the top of Northern Territory.

* * *

Darwin

When I was in Australia in 2001–02, the authorities were still procrastinating over whether or not to build a train line from Alice Springs to Darwin. I'm reliably informed that the line is now complete but back then I didn't have the luxury of the train. I had to rely on the bus to get me to Darwin, and it was an eighteen-hour ride, dry and uncomfortable.

I arrived as evening was falling and the bus driver showed me the way to the nearby hostel. It was a small place with a big reception area. I was shown around and reached my dorm without falling into the pool. The hostel was centrally situated, with a pub next door!

I immediately enquired about excursions and learnt that Darwin is notable for two things: firstly, it's home to Australia's pearl industry and secondly, it was battered by a cyclone in 1974–75, which caused much damage. There were city tours that pass museums including Army, Pearl and Air; also an evening harbour tour on an old pearl lugger, which included wine. Finally, I enquired about a crocodile tour to a national park.

I began my city tour the next day around 11 am and finished around 4 pm. The bus had open windows as I was now in the tropics with hot, sticky, humid weather; I sweated constantly. I visited a reptile farm where I witnessed the crocodiles being fed. There were several lying in the sun. The normal length of an adult male Saltwater crocodile, the largest of the species, is 15-18ft (4.1-5.5 metres) – although mature males can grow to 20ft (6 metres). Crocodiles tend to congregate in fresh-water rivers, lakes and swamps – although they also inhabit saltwater areas. They are carnivorous and ambush their prey. In Australia they are protected and live in the outback of Northern Territory, Queensland and the northern part of Western Australia

The ones we saw were in a pool protected from the public by wire fences. Their keeper passed in pieces of meat on the end of a long pole. An adult male crocodile leapt and hit the fence yards from where I was standing. It was a powerful motion that shook the whole cage. Afterwards, a baby crocodile was passed around the group. Its mouth was taped to prevent it from biting. The female lays three large eggs annually. This crocodile was about 1 ft (30 cm) long, was heavy, muscular, and wriggled aggressively. Its upper skin was hard and tough, yet its underbelly was soft. The four claws were razor sharp. It felt fantastic to hold one. I relinquished the crocodile reluctantly, and it was passed around until a small boy dropped it, whereupon the reptile shot away in the vain hope of escape.

Next I headed back into town on the tour bus to the Pearl Museum. An electric storm erupted and everyone on the bus got soaked. The rain evaporated immediately and the heat and humidity returned. We passed by a hotel where a small car had been picked up during a cyclone and dumped into an upstairs swimming pool – it was still there!

At the Pearl Museum I sat through a twenty-minute technical documentary about how pearls were formed and lugged. I had a quick tour around and was allowed to feel some pearls, including a half mother pearl. It is the unique and rare oyster pearl, which is the gem that divers seek, and is most sought after by the rich. As the weather was misbehaving, I intended to head back to the hostel. However, before I returned, I visited the Air Museum.

The Japanese in WWII had bombed the Australian northern coastal towns of Broom and Darwin. Indeed, at one point, it appeared that the Japanese might invade. The US Air Force loaned the Australians many planes and used various Pacific islands to attack the Japanese in the final phase of the war. For service during and after the war, the US government gave the Australian Air Force a B52 bomber. These planes began service after WWII and were used during the Cold War.

The plane in the museum protected the skies during the 1950s and 1960s. She was a magnificent aircraft and I walked around her, passing under her huge wings. I ran my cane along one wing to get an idea of her size – she was massive! I listened to a documentary about her before taking a tour around the remainder of the museum. I spent a happy hour there, hearing war stories of the Australian Air Force and glad to have met an American B52.

I had to visit the hospital on the far side of town for another blood test to check up on my kidney problem. One of the hostel staff gave me a ride. I presented my documentation to a doctor and was examined. My blood pressure was still extremely high and I was given more medication.

Around 5 pm the hostel ran a trip to the harbour to feed Milkfish – this cost $5. I stood in the shallows with the evening sun on my back, feeding the smooth, slimy fish.

Later that evening I was driven to another part of Darwin's large harbour and boarded a long, narrow pearl lugger. There were two young guys in charge who gave everyone a glass of wine. To enter the harbour, we first had to exit a canal lock gate. We heard all about diving, how the oysters formed the pearls and how they were stored and carried by the lugger. The young guys told us that Darwin is one of the World's largest natural harbours, although I was beginning to realise that all the harbour trips say that so it's hard to tell which one is accurate! The three hour trip was relaxing and I felt the hot sun on my back as it went down and the wind on my face as it came off the sea. We chugged along listening to the tour guides. If the tour is still running, I'd highly recommend it.

A group of us went on a full day excursion to Kakadu National Park. At the breakfast stop, we were given the day's itinerary, and someone brought in a dingo, which I was able to touch. The animal was placid and furry. A guy played the piano and the dingo howled – apparently they can't bark!

At the park, we went on a hike which involved climbing up several rocks, but I wasn't allowed to climb because the guide wouldn't take the responsibility for my safety. I could have done it easily enough, but you have to respect other people's judgement when they have a large group to look after.

The undulating trail passed through rocks and bush, where there was little shelter from the hot sun. We stopped for lunch and I was able to touch several animal exhibits, including a turtle shell and a stuffed crocodile. We took a boat ride through the park, and the pilot let me steer the boat. This was fantastic! I helmed, just keeping the speed steady and driving straight for about ten minutes. It was a relaxing ride, and there was a range of different native birds. Some crocodiles were spotted in the water and one or two were lying in the sun. The riverbanks were lined with bush and at one point we spotted a snake near the water's edge.

On the journey back to Darwin, we stopped at Gagudju Crocodile Hotel, a large building whose entrance represents a croc's mouth. I entered and the guide showed me a statue of a large crocodile chasing a fish. I arrived back at the hostel around 10 pm after having dinner at a restaurant that was included in the price of my trip.

On my final day in town, I went to an animal park. I had trouble organising this as it was a self-guided park, but I was able to pay extra for a personal guide. The park resembled a zoo, and my guide drove the bus and went in with me. She was young and friendly, like everyone I met in Darwin. I was able to hold a koala bear, which was usually forbidden because the marsupial could catch infections from human hands. He sniffed me and climbed up my chest. Most people believe koalas are cuddly, but up close they can be vicious. They have sharp teeth and claws, and if attacked they would retaliate fiercely.

Next, we went to feed 'Skippy' the kangaroo. I was able to touch a Joey – a baby kangaroo. The mother was docile, which seemed strange for such a large animal. I was given a snake to hold and I placed it around my neck; this one was really thick and strong. It moved around me for a few minutes and then I handed it back. Touching the animals and getting close to nature was a wonderful experience. I felt very privileged.

My next stop was Cairns in north Queensland, which was a forty hour bus journey away. I was heading to the east coast for more adventures!

Chapter 6

The Coast of Australia

Australia has four enormous coasts, each with their own wonders and fascinations. However, the east coast has the most attractions and is the easiest to travel. Therefore, it made sense to head east for Cairns rather than the west coast, which is largely barren.

To get to Cairns from Darwin, I had two choices: I could travel overland on a small bus and sleep in the bush for one fee, or I could take the Greyhound bus. The latter took the long way around, but was slightly cheaper. I opted for the Greyhound because it ran daily while the mini-bus only left on certain days.

The journey from Darwin to Cairns took just over forty-four hours. The route went half way back to Alice Springs before I had to change buses and go north-east in a slow curve, which took me through the outback of Northern Queensland and eventually to Cairns. It was a hot and dusty, bumpy ride that was sore on the body, but I was glad for the experience. This was my first lengthy journey overland and I found it thrilling – over 2,000 miles (3,000 km). The bus drivers were generally friendly, hard but fair.

The journey was non-eventful except for one incident.

After about twelve hours of travelling at breakneck speed, we stopped at a small town in the bush to get petrol and clean the bus. We were told to alight and had to stand in the middle of the outback on our own at 3 am. Although it was humid, there was a slight breeze. Suddenly, out of the silence of the Victoria Desert, came a loud howl as a pack of dingoes began their call. It pierced the night, scaring everyone!

Cairns

I was nearing the end of my first month in Australia, all was going swimmingly and I was enjoying myself immensely. After checking in at the hostel, I was directed to a nearby restaurant. I had fish, called Barramundi, which tasted plain so I washed it down with a few drinks. I had changed beer once again and was now drinking Tilly's. Cairns is in the tropics and constantly humid; the nights were almost unbearable.

The next morning, I enquired at the travel desk about activities, and booked a sky dive, white water rafting, trips to an animal sanctuary and the Great Barrier Reef.

The dorms at this hostel were in an open yard and I had to find my way from outside to get to the reception area. A lady in her forties collected six backpackers and myself and we took a short drive to the animal sanctuary and park.

We fed the kangaroos with hard seed; I stroked them and felt another Joey. We listened to an hour-long talk about the many animals and birds that lived at the wild life sanctuary. During the talk a small wallaby was passed around – when I held him he sat on my lap and wriggled. Most of the animals were rescued and cared for by the sanctuary, and the babies were bottle fed to begin with. Next, the lady produced a baby koala that tried to bite her fingers. She said that koalas were normally shy and didn't like to be touched or stared at. Koala is an aborigine word meaning water drinking; they too are marsupials, not bears, as most people believe. We were told that we shouldn't stroke them with our hands, but rub their fur with our knuckles, and also not to touch their heads as this frightens them.

I woke late the next day and went in search of breakfast, the only thing the Australian hostels didn't provide. I prepared for my sky dive. It was a Tuesday and it was Melbourne Cup Day, a national horse race, celebrated countrywide. Large parts of the country grind to a standstill. People bet on the horses, and ladies dress up in their finery. The Melbourne Cup is shown on TV in bars, everywhere. It's a huge event – but I went sky diving instead!

Along with three other guys, I was driven out to the airstrip, met in the hanger by the crew and was kitted out with a jumpsuit and helmet. I had to sign a health and safety form, which also declared that I had no medical conditions – I lied about my kidneys and took a chance. I was on the east coast now and the fun was just about to begin. Next I was instructed how to sky dive. A guy sat behind me, put my arms across my chest and said on the count of three to roll forward; we tried this several times until the instructor thought I was ready. I pointed out that I wouldn't be able to hear, as I had to remove my hearing aids, so he said he would tap me. The instructors were very confident and amusing. This was my first sky dive, so I didn't know what to expect, but my adrenocortico-trophic hormones were beginning to flow!

The tandem sky dive cost me $280 dollars (£110), about half what it would cost in the UK, and we were jumping from 14,000 ft (4,600 metres). They asked me if I wanted oxygen. I smiled and declined. Four of us piled into the small plane, and I asked if I could have a go at flying – they agreed. We climbed quickly and when we were around 10,000 ft (3,300 metres) I slid into the co-pilot's seat and for half a minute handled the controls. This was thrilling. I tried to waggle the wings, but then I had to relinquish control. The experience was brief but electrifying.

I had been told that just before it was time to jump, I would be attached to my partner who had the parachutes. He told me that there were two parachutes per person. He shouted to me once "Ready?"

I replied, "Yes." I was sweating like a pig, the adrenalin was flowing, and I was a little scared and very excited.

We were strapped together, I removed my hearing aids and the aircraft door was opened. I felt the cold air hit the cabin and my body began to shake. I didn't quite know what to expect – would my blood pressure go sky high and give me a heart attack? How would I breathe? We were 14,000 ft (4,600 metres) up when this suddenly occurred to me! Then I was pushed to the opening. It was now or never. There was no turning back.

I sat on the edge, the strong force of the wind tried to suck me out. I got my legs out, crossed my arms and reclined my head. After three taps, we rolled forward and dropped...

Bang, we were out! All 14 stone (89 kg) of me and my 12 stone (76 kg) partner, the two of us dropping, freefalling like a stone.

I hit the air, which felt like slamming into water. I circled continuously, breathing fast, in and out, like a whale that has surfaced for oxygen. I can't do justice to the description of the sensation, except to say that it was incredible. I felt warm sun as well as the coolness of the wind. We dropped fast, freefalling from 14,000 to 4,000 ft (4,600 to 1,300 metres) in just over sixty seconds.

Abruptly, my partner pulled the parachute and the pain began. I was yanked unceremoniously from a horizontal position to a vertical one, and jerked upright when the harness straps bit into my legs. It was sudden and without warning! I managed to adjust the straps and get some degree of comfort while we were swinging across the sky over Cairns' beaches. I was given a hearing aid 4,000 ft (1,300 metres) above the ground, and I shouted with happy delirium. The feeling was tremendous. We were flying! I was able to control the parachute and with my partner's help we circled around, lined up and then swooped down.

A few more swoops and we approached for the landing. At this point, I was told to get my legs up and keep them straight, which is absolutely vital because failing to do this could result in a broken leg on landing. My partner said, "Get them up, Tony," as we came in over the beach. One bump and a drag across the sand, and I was down on my backside.

We'd made it. What a thrill!

I shouted, "Oh shit, man! Wahoo!"

When I returned to the hostel, the girls at reception asked me how it was and all I could say was, "Fucking great!"

The next morning I was driven to the rafting base on the Tully River, an hour and a half south of Cairns. The water levels of the river are constant, allowing for good rafting. I met the crew and the two guides and was given a wetsuit. We turned them inside out so that they were white, because apparently this would stop the sand flies from landing on us. Mosquitoes had already bitten me, but that was nothing compared to the sand flies! They were large, with a painful bite, and could be found along the entire coast.

In our group there was a couple from England and a German guy. We were equipped with helmet, paddle and life jacket, carried the raft down to the river and all climbed aboard. I got a place near the back and had one instructor behind me. He was a noisy but friendly Aussie who kept hitting my back to kill the sand flies and teased me all day, although I returned as much as he dished out.

As soon as we were in the raft and on the river, we were instructed how to paddle and steer the craft. We got to grips with the commands – and then we were off!

We paddled down-river in serene surroundings of rocks and bush. Events began gently; we passed through a couple of small rapids with no trouble, but after forty minutes on the river, we had our first large one, a Rapid 4. Rapids are graded 1 to 5 in their size and danger, with 1 being the gentlest and 5 the largest and most severe. We entered the large rapid hard and ran left, almost colliding with a rock on our way. I managed to escape most of the water. Then we were into it, it was high fives with the paddles and we commenced down river. It was hard work and hot. I had an English lady next to me who I almost hit in the face with my paddle end; we swore at each other and got wet. My feet were permanently submerged after we hit the first big rapid. I wore sun cream but it was useless in the water. My arms were sunburnt and my fingers were blistered, but I didn't care. After several rapids, and getting wet again descending another Rapid 4, we all jumped into the river for refreshment. I wore my analogue hearing aids, I have to, and took a chance with the water. We pulled over about half way through the forty-four rapids and had lunch in the rain forest. Our picnic spot was swarming with sand flies, which made eating a hamburger quite difficult.

On the second part of the course, we had to negotiate a large rock that split the river; it had on it an Aborigine painting. Getting past the rock was fun, we had to rely on our guide to give the right information and read the rapid correctly, or we would be in the drink! This almost happened more than once, and did occur on this occasion. We paddled hard on the left to get around the huge rock, but on going through a series of boulders on the approach to a medium size rapid, our guide read the turn wrong. We almost got through the major part of the rapid, but he said paddle right when it should have been left and almost everyone, except me, went in the water! The girl on my right grabbed hold of my arm, then suddenly remembered that I should not go in. It was a hilarious moment. I had attempted to push the guides in all day, and finally succeeded!

The final series of rapids had us really working, as they were rather large. The third from the end excited everyone and I got a drenching; one of my hearing aids packed up but the other one, although troublesome, continued to work. At the end, we ran into a wall of water. We came through it, had a huge high five with our paddles and headed to the shore.

It was all a great laugh; tiring, but fun. Doing this activity with other people was fantastic. I learnt so much about myself – what I could achieve, how people reacted to me, and how my humour was accepted. We returned to the boathouse where I changed and had a couple of beers. For anybody visiting Cairns I would strongly recommend this fantastic activity.

I was knackered, but there was still more to come! The next morning I was woken up and told, "Tony, time to go to the Great Barrier Reef."

I groaned, pulled on my previous night's clothes, got a towel and my swimming trunks and ran down to get the bus to take me to the harbour. Once there, I was helped aboard a large yacht and taken out to the Barrier Reef. Everybody was ordered into groups, told to put on wetsuits and get into lines. We were allowed into the water to snorkel or dive on the reef. I went snorkelling; I figured water pressure was more damaging on my body than air pressure and I had my ears to consider.

Again, I had to complete a form, but this time I declared my high blood pressure. I put on the wetsuit, flippers, snorkel and mask and, along with a crew member, entered the water and snorkelled around for about an hour, holding onto a rubber ring.

I was allowed down to touch the reef briefly, which was really kind. I'd touched reef coral while I was in Darwin and knew its rough texture. I had to be careful because a coral reef is a living eco system and touching it could damage the organisms.

The guy who looked after me brought up a sea caterpillar for me to touch. It felt like a large worm. Apparently, it feeds and excretes from the same hole! I also felt a large, hard starfish. After an hour's snorkelling we all climbed back aboard the yacht.

On our way back to the harbour we were given t-shirts and as we docked our guide asked if we'd had a good day and we made as much noise as possible. I yelled at the top of my lungs! It was a long day and again I got sunburnt; that Australian sun is damned hot and very dangerous if you are not careful.

This was my last event in Cairns as I was heading off for pastures new, but for other travellers there is so much more to see and do. Townsville and Cape Tribulation are in the near vicinity, and further north is Cape York Peninsular. However, I needed to be moving down the coast – I had so much more to explore!

I asked one of the hostel receptionists to help me plan the next leg of my trip. She organised my entire itinerary as far as Brisbane – transport, accommodation and activities. I was extremely grateful to her, as she helped me enormously and made travelling so much easier for me.

Airlie Beach and Whitsunday Islands
I journeyed to Airlie Beach, some eight hours drive down the coast. An elderly couple owned the small

hostel I stayed at and it had a large bar with wooden panels. I telephoned the Sailing Company to check on my three-day cruise to the Whitsunday Islands off the north Queensland coast. I wanted to ensure that it was still running, discover the collection point and what gear I needed. A company administrator told me, in no uncertain terms, what to bring and the departure time. I asked if they could pick me up from the hostel, and they agreed to pass nearby.

I was collected and we set off for the port. At the harbour, I headed towards the boat with about fifteen other travellers. One of the crew introduced himself and we went to a shop on the jetty to stock up for the trip – I just bought alcohol.

I grabbed a batch of forty beers and as I was paying, an Australian lady said in a rough voice, "Hey, what's your name?"

I replied, "Tony."

She said, "Hi, I'm a blonde, blue eyed, big-boobed girl and I'm the cook!"

Once aboard the yacht, we gathered in the saloon, down three small steps. The blonde lady in her mid-twenties gave us a talk. She told us that we were sailing to several of the islands for three days, and we would need lots of sun cream and a hat. There were plenty of drinks on board so we just made a tab and wrote down our names. She told us to remove our footwear whilst on board and then showed everyone to his or her bunks – I had a sofa bed in the saloon.

The boat was a large twin sail yacht, about 90 ft (30 metres) long. There were three crew members, the skipper, the deckhand who had helped me aboard, and the cook. The yacht was quite spacious; someone asked if they could sleep on deck and the lady gave permission.

There are numerous islands along Australia's north-eastern coast and the Whitsunday Islands are among the most delightful. The young deckhand showed me around the boat and demonstrated the workings of the sails. He and I laughed together and had lots of fun. The passengers were permitted to sail the vessel but my assistance was limited as the crew thought this to be too dangerous. Therefore, I spent most of my time sitting under the main sail, drinking beer and/or water and lapping up the sun.

The first day was spent sailing to the islands. We lounged around on deck, listening to music on the stereo and getting to know one another. There were several couples, a few from the US, an English couple Sue and John, and a guy named Mike from Liverpool. The Aussie lady and I had a few laughs during the adventure; I chased her into her galley at one point! She kept telling all the girls I wanted my body rubbed with sun cream – and several obliged!

We anchored in a bay after around six hours sailing and some of the group went for a swim. I got my bearings around the boat and had discovered the icebox where the beer was stored. I helped myself to quite a few of my stow and got mighty drunk. The sun was scorching, I was surrounded by lovely girls and the scenery was fantastic – the open expanse of clear water with no one else around to spoil the view or peace. The smell of the sea and the quietness of the open expanse were delicious to the body's senses. I could detect the gentle energy of my environment and it was magical.

Later that evening the Aussie lady and the young guy disappeared in a small inflatable boat to visit a friend. I chatted with the skipper, who was in his forties and had been sailing for around twenty years. He said he was impressed by my inclination for adventure and my independence. I had several more beers and he left me there, turning out all the lights on the boat.

Later the Aussie lady said, "Tony won't be able to see, 'cause all the lights are out," before realising that I was blind to begin with!

We had an early breakfast, which I only just managed to wake up for. Apparently I'd snored like a freight train all night and had driven several people out on deck. I didn't really care because I was a selfish, arrogant bastard back then. We began the day by having a swim and a snorkel. I fell off the end of the boat into the sea and swam around, enjoying the coolness of the water on my hot body.

The Whitsunday Islands are blessed with some of the World's most exquisite beaches, many of them untouched by humans, which make a pleasant change. We sailed around many of the islands and found a good spot, launched the inflatable and ferried the group to White-haven beach. The inflatable hit each wave with such ferocity that I felt the impact traverse my spine. The ride was sensational, the fresh, sea air tickling my nostrils – the strong salt wind slapping my face, causing a sharp grating upon my cheeks and nose. Each crash of the inflatable on the waves was like a new roller coaster ride, an unexpected excitement. My entire body was bounced up and down, side to side, every muscle screaming with each descent of the small craft.

The islands were lined with sharp coral and were difficult to reach. We had around an hour on each one. The young Aussie guy and I put on flippers and went for a swim, but I found the current too strong and with coral everywhere, I couldn't put my feet down. Several of the group said they saw turtles and small dolphins. There were reef sharks about, but they weren't very dangerous. The crystal beach was amazing, unbelievable white sand that reflected the sun glaringly, and was hot to the touch and very fine. I felt privileged to be there.

We returned to the yacht and sailed on; we had to get to a bay inlet before sundown. When we arrived, I opened more beer and relaxed with the crew. The beach bar we headed to that night forbade footwear. The evening began early, as I sat in the cockpit near the icebox, drinking and telling rude jokes.

After about two hours of this, we went to the beach bar where I managed to get exceedingly drunk. The Aussie guys got me back to the yacht, I slipped on the deck trying to climb aboard and fell into the inflatable. I awoke the next morning as breakfast was finishing. I had wanted to helm the boat, but our skipper had forgotten the day before, so now he let me. I stood on the platform at the yachts stern with the large wooden wheel in my hands and kept the vessel on a steady course.

However, even with a t-shirt on and a towel around my shoulders, I was still unable to cope with the intense heat. After about fifty minutes of this, I started to feel I was being burnt, so I relinquished the helm and found some shade. We stopped at one more island before we sailed back to Airlie Beach and the Australian mainland.

That evening I was hurting a little, my back ached and was badly sunburnt, as were my arms and legs. I met up with Mike and another guy and went to the pub to meet the others; this was a Whitsunday crew ritual. We had all been given t-shirts on this trip and I was wearing mine. It looked cool, the white reflecting off my sunburn. The bar was noisy, the food somewhat expensive. Conversation was difficult because of the noise. I met the skipper and the other Aussie guy. Later the place turned into a karaoke, and we had a laugh before going our separate ways.

Hervey Bay and Fraser Island
I next went on to Hervey Bay, which was a six-hour bus journey along the coast.

The hostel had a bar/restaurant, and the dorms were separated from the main building by a garden. It was a big place and there were plenty of people. I arrived around early evening, settled in and got my bearings before turning in for the night.

The next morning, a guy in a 4 x 4 vehicle collected nine of us, and we took a ferry to the large sandy island called Fraser, off the coast of central Queensland. Horses run wild on the island and often whales and dolphins can be seen. The group included a young Scottish couple who I got to know, and some English girls who I chatted up. We had a two-day tour, spending one night on Fraser Island sleeping in huts. I sat in the front of the vehicle with the driver-guide, who told us about the island as he drove. We did a couple of hikes, one through some trees on the hot, soft sand. You could hire your own vehicle and drive around the sand dunes independently if you wished, but only in a group of four because Fraser Island isn't a place for the inexperienced. The sand dunes can do damage to any non-four-wheel-drive car, and people who are unused to such a vehicle usually become stuck in the sand. There were snakes on the island and dingoes. The dingoes usually leave people alone, but the snakes don't! Apparently, the previous year, a snake had killed a three-year-old boy in his tent. The heat is another danger, and also losing your bearings – a frequent habit of tourists and young backpackers!

The trees afforded us some shelter from the blazing sun. We all climbed a large sand dune that gave us a good view out to sea. This was where the horses ran wild, and where whales had been spotted, but there were none swimming by when we were there. The hut we stayed in was in the middle of the island; there was a pub, of course, and a barbeque.

We hit camp around 7 pm after a long and tiring day. I immediately went in search of the pub, which I found after getting lost crossing a grassy area. The barman was humorous, tough and had large hands; we swapped many stories. I later returned to the camp where a barbecue was cooking. We had steak and sausage to eat and I kept the party amused with adventurous tales. This allowed our guide to go and have a good night's sleep.

The next day, we made our way to a huge sand hill, which eventually led us down to the sea after a long and tiring walk. We all dived in. The sand bank just kept going. I stood in the water with the Scottish guy and another English guy, talking and laughing. They were winding me up. We were there for about an hour before we took a walk over the scorching sand and eventually had a well-earned lunch in the shade of some trees. Whilst we were eating, several kookaburras came and stole some food. One bird even took a sausage from a girl, just as she was putting it in her mouth!

After lunch, we went for a wander through the woods. The Scottish guy and I crept up on a Kookaburra and I touched its tail; it didn't flinch.

There were two options for returning to Hervey Bay: we could travel by ferry or take a small aeroplane. The English girls, another guy and myself chose to fly. We took off and swooped low over the bay and eventually over Hervey. I asked if I could fly the plane and the pilot said he would love to allow me, but not with passengers.

On landing, we waited for the remainder of the group to arrive and then we all said our goodbyes. I was off on the next leg of my trip!

Brisbane

On waking around midday, I quickly packed and caught the bus for the very long journey to Brisbane, Queensland's capital city. I arrived at a large transportation centre, which was busy and confusing. I didn't know the way to the hostel, so took a taxi. The hostel was a strange building; the reception was a round shaped area and this disorientated me more than once. The hostel was disappointing, as it was in a poor location and, although it was near the transportation centre, it was far from the city centre or any food outlets. They had a café, but that closed early. There were few people there and all the reception staff were offhand, except for one guy. I did two excursions. The first was an all-day city tour which included a visit to a sheep farm where I purchased a money pouch made from a kangaroo's testicle! My second trip took me to a rainforest national park some way from Brisbane. I was collected early, along with two girls from England and a couple of other guys. The guide was an unusual man with a strange, high-pitched accent. He asked us all questions like where we were from and what was our most interesting travel story? I told the tale of having my flip-flops exchanged in Melbourne.

We drove out of Brisbane for about two hours, along some mountain paths that wound through a small village where we stopped for breakfast. I felt the twists of the mountain as we ascended, and noticed the change in altitude as the air became fresher and cooler. The village was small and quiet. At the national park we walked down approximately two hundred rough steps that varied in size, onto a trail that took us through the rainforest. We saw a couple of spiders sleeping on a large leaf; luckily, they weren't Black Widow or Red Back. We didn't see any snakes, but I suspected there were plenty around. The rainforest felt moist after the day's heat and humidity. The terrain under foot was soft, dry earth and twigs. The trail got tougher as we encountered rocks and boulders. We passed a stream and eventually came upon a number of large boulders and rocks that led to a large waterfall. I had to climb over the rocks and negotiate my way around to a good seat. Some of the rocks were rough and large, several were wet and slippery – the area smelt earthy and natural; it was a peaceful place.

We stayed for about ten minutes enjoying the tranquillity of the waterfall before heading back. Once we were near to the top of the trail where the steps began, the guide left us so that he could set up lunch. The rest of us found a rock pool and dived in. There was a small waterfall at the far end, but I just stayed on the edge, not wanting to get my hearing aids wet. We had lunch in a park and returned to the city, stopping in another small mountain village for ice cream.

Brisbane has many attractions, mainly the Brisbane River, which I experienced on my city tour. It's pleasant and a meeting area for many locals. The city hosted the Commonwealth Games in 1984 and its sports complexes are excellent. I decided against visiting the Brisbane cricket ground, known as the Gabba, since there was no tour. Brisbane also has a large zoo that contains a huge reptile collection, which apparently is well worth visiting.

I by-passed the Gold Coast region and headed towards Byron Bay in the State of New South Wales (NSW).

Byron Bay
It took a good eight hours to get to Byron from Brisbane. I arrived late in the afternoon and stayed two nights. I enquired what Byron had to offer, and the lady who owned the hostel told me that I could go sky diving, bungee jumping or hand and para-gliding. Someone had told me about a nearby town called Nimbin, which had an 'alternative' culture. I booked a trip to Nimbin for the next day.

I went for a para-glide, which cost around $40.

I was given a helmet and strapped into a buggy seat at the back of the para-glider and we took off. We climbed to about 4,000 ft (1,300 metres) and flew over the ocean. The engine was incredibly loud. I was able to waggle the wings a few times and we swooped around at a fast speed for about twenty minutes, before returning to earth.

The next day began smoothly enough; about a dozen people and I were driven to various locations. We visited a couple of lookouts and some coastal buildings. We stopped in Nimbin for lunch which is a small inland town about an hour's drive from Byron Bay and, just as I'd been told, it really is a place of alternative culture. The driver told us that each person who passed us on the street would offer to sell us hash-cakes and/or pot. I just wanted to sit in a café and eat the cakes. The driver left me in a cafe and returned to collect me about an hour later. I had two cakes on an empty stomach and took two more with me. It hit me some time later, when I began to get stoned.

Draft dodgers of the Vietnam War established this culture at the beginning of the 1970s. They went to Nimbin and created a hippy town, full of pot and cafes.

We visited a park and the driver put me on a bench to get some fresh air. It was at this point that I thought I could see lights going round in front of me; it was a funny sensation. I had one more cake when I returned to the hostel and felt happy, but slightly faint and very light headed. It was a good, crazy feeling.

Sydney
It was getting hot as I approached Sydney; it was nearly

December and the Australian summer was well established.

I took a taxi from the bus station to the hostel as it was a long walk and I didn't know the way. The hostel was a tower block in Glebe Point, reasonably priced and had friendly staff. The place was busy, as you would expect in Sydney. The hostel had a basement with a tiny kitchen and a rooftop area. There was a table tennis table in the basement that I later found out was mostly used for various kinds of sex, including multiple partners!

I became friendly with some of the female staff and they told me how to get in and out of the city by bus. I planned five days in Sydney, as I had been told that it was a great place. Personally I found it overrated – although the bridge, the harbour and the Opera House do certainly conjure up a vivid picture. Sydney is complicated, unlike Melbourne. It's not on a grid system but shaped around the natural harbour and has vast suburbs. The city has its good points; there are many attractions and a thriving night life. I wanted a tour around the Opera House plus a harbour excursion, and the Blue Mountain trip was a must!

I wandered around Sydney a little frustrated, as I knew my destination but it was difficult getting anywhere, and I found the events I undertook unsatisfactory. For instance, I took a harbour cruise one night and even though we passed under the bridge, I failed to get any impression of it. Whether that was because it was dark, or due to my blindness, I'm not sure. The fact that the Olympics had been there a year earlier produced an over-impressive image that sadly didn't fulfil my expectations. Nevertheless, I was lucky to be there and I did get a nice surprise one evening when I walked around Darling Harbour. I was minding my own business, enjoying the cool evening air and the sound of the sea, when a voice shouted, "Hey, Tony!"

I was startled and nearly fell backwards into the water! It was the Scottish couple I had met on Fraser Island. They had spotted and recognised me. I greeted them and we went for some drinks and dinner. They had their bikes with them and were staying at a campsite. We had ice cream near the harbour and I enjoyed the cool evening, catching up on events.

I discovered the Opera House conducted guided tours, and caught a bus into the city from in front of the hostel. The tour lasted about an hour and was very informative. I'd highly recommend it. I learnt that the Opera House is divided into four main auditoriums, with an area for chamber music, a main opera hall and two smaller rooms. The roof is constructed in the shape of a sail. Although the building is mainly for opera and classical music, both the band Crowded House and comedian Billy Connelly have performed there.

As for the bridge, that was a disaster! I enquired whether they would let a blind person climb it, but the company refused point blank – they wouldn't even consider my request. I could have argued on the grounds of discrimination, but it was not worth the hassle. This was the only time in Australia I had any such problems. Otherwise, the Australians were kind, good-natured, humorous and usually very helpful.

The best event I undertook while in Sydney was my excursion to the Blue Mountains, which is an absolute-must trip, even if you only have two days in Sydney. This was an all-day event that gave a quick city tour, before driving through the suburbs. Once out of the city, there was continuous vegetation, which smelt fresh and delightful. We were in open countryside and climbing, though we did stop briefly for breakfast. On entering the mountains, the view and scenery changed from roads and bare bush to hills, green countryside, trees with leaves and clean air – it was also very hot. At our second stop, I was given a baby rock wallaby to hold. It was small and wrapped up inside a cloth bag. The women cooed over the baby!

We searched for some high vantage points to look at the mountains. There were several places to see the mountain range, which is a sandstone plateau 3,400 ft (1,199 metres) above sea level. You could look down in places to the forest below. Our guide told us that if we looked across the area space of the valley, it appeared possible to cross it in an hour or two. One man tried to do it, and some four days later, he crawled out on the other side! He was unrecognisable as a human being as his body was covered with leaches and his features were emaciated. Anybody who goes into the bush, or jungle as it was there, could get easily lost, and the creatures who live in that habitat do nasty things to human flesh!

We drove to another vantage point at a place known as 'The Three Sisters'. There is a trio of mountains together that, when viewed closely, resemble the shape of three women – hence the name! I found it peaceful up there, away from the noise of the city, the fumes and the people. The guide told us that some vegetation had recently been discovered in the Blue Mountains, which pre-dated dinosaurs. There is so much unexplored bush and forest, nobody knows what other discoveries might be found.

We climbed several hills with steps to get to vantage points – it was good exercise for my alcohol-ridden body. The air was much cleaner and thinner. We drove for long periods up various hills, and I noticed the change in gradient. I enjoyed a fantastic day amongst nature.

The following day I caught the bus to Canberra, the country's capital, in the Australian Capital Territory (ACT).

Canberra

Canberra is a man-made city between Melbourne and Sydney. It was created in the 1920s to defuse the argument regarding Australia's capital.

I booked a hostel out of the city, in the bush. I arrived after a three-hour bus ride and took a taxi to the hostel. It was late in the evening and the only food available was take-away. The girl who worked there was extremely friendly, young and chatty. I only had two days in the capital and I discovered this was enough. The following day the young guy on reception offered to give me a ride into town.

Canberra is a quiet, pleasant city with a triangular lake in the middle. There are two Houses of Parliament, an old one and a new one. The reception guy took me to the modern House of Parliament and I joined a one-hour tour. The Australian Parliament consists of two representatives from each of the six states, and the two territories Northern Territory and ACT. I visited the parliament room where the Queen of England had stood during her last visit. The Australian people had recently voted in a referendum to keep the Queen as their figurehead.

I visited the War Museum on my second and final day. It is divided into various sections, and rivals the Imperial War Museum in London. A young male guide took me on an hour's tour, and allowed me to climb into a jeep and an anti-aircraft gun. There was a wall memorial with the crest of each state beside the names. An older lady took me around for two hours. There were caps and insignia from a British General of WWII, Percy Montgomery. There were also photos and letters from the Australian 'heroes' who went to destroy enemy ships in Singapore harbour. Many were captured and killed on the second raid. Their first effort was spectacular!

I returned to Sydney where I caught another bus to Brisbane, which took about twenty-eight hours altogether. I slept most of the way. In Brisbane, I went to the airport and boarded a plane to the next leg of my journey... New Zealand!

Chapter 7

Travelling the Islands of New Zealand

North Island

The New Zealand islands are a volcanic beauty, wonderful and magical. I discovered this in just under twelve weeks of travelling around by bus, mostly incredibly drunk. I had a blast, met fantastic people and undertook crazy events. New Zealand was the natural country to explore after Australia. It's only a five hour flight away, and I was able to use my Australian visa.

I knew little about New Zealand, except that they play cricket and that rugby is not just the national sport – it's a religion! I had a rough plan to start my journey in Auckland, and end in Christchurch. I wanted to reach Stewart Island, a place visited by very few.

Auckland

I flew from Brisbane to Auckland on the east of New Zealand's North Island on 3rd December 2001. I arrived in the early evening and as I was being escorted through customs I heard a lady say, 'please' and 'thank you' in the same sentence. I said, "Can you repeat that, I've just come from Australia?"

I took the airport shuttle bus into the city; I'd already

reserved a hostel whilst I was in Sydney, which I'd booked for five nights. New Zealand currency was $3.3 to the £1. The hostel was on a hill near the centre; there were several bars and a red light district nearby. It was a relaxing place, and had a large reception area with a travel desk. After familiarising myself with the building the receptionist gave me directions to some food outlets. I found a pub, entered, went to the bar and ordered a beer. I was offered a choice of Black Lion or Red Lion, amongst others.

I asked for a local beer and on tasting it, said, "This will do, mate," sat on a bar stool and absorbed the atmosphere.

The pub was large with many people watching the cricket on TV. New Zealand were playing a test match against Australia and it appeared that New Zealand were winning. I had a meal and stayed until closing time.

At the travel desk I enquired about available excursions and conversed with a lovely local girl. I liked her voice and easy accent. There were several options: the usual city bus tour, and the possibility of swimming with dolphins in the bay. I chose the city tour, which was interesting and informative.

I alighted from the bus at one point to stretch my legs and walked around one of the harbours and breathed in some fresh New Zealand air.

I finished my day with a guided tour around the war museum. The building was divided into different sections, with the main part concentrating on New Zealand's efforts in World War I and World War II. There were memorials dedicated to the various forces of the Auckland region that had served during the wars in which New Zealand participated, namely WWI, WWII, Korea and Vietnam. I found this fascinating. On the ground floor of the museum there were a couple of tanks and several different aeroplanes suspended from the ceiling. I discovered, to my amazement, that during WWII a Japanese submarine reached as far as New Zealand's South Island.

Auckland is divided into two halves by a large bay. Circa 1840 European immigrants began arriving in this area. The city was created as a British colonial settlement after 3,000 acres of land – present day central Auckland City – was purchased from the Ngati Whatua Tribe. It briefly became the capital of New Zealand, principally for its two harbours, fertile land and river access to the whole of North Island. Within a year nearly 2,000 people were living in hastily constructed accommodation, many near the harbours or on the small isthmus.

Today, the central part of the urban area still occupies the isthmus which lies between Manukau Harbour on the Tasman Sea and Whaitenata Harbour on the Pacific Ocean. Auckland is one of the few cities in the world to have two harbours situated on two separate major bodies of water. Bridges join both harbours.

I was chilling in my room one evening when I met a cool English guy. We went out for a few beers and he described the girls to me. I really appreciated the service!

My bush tour was intriguing. I was collected around 8.30 am and, along with several other hostellers, we drove into the countryside. The female guide was half Maori and half European. The Maori are descendents of Polynesian people who, arguably, arrived in the islands circa 950 AD. We drove for a good two hours stopping at several places to enjoy the scenery. The weather was damp and cold.

The guide told us about New Zealand's European history. Able Tasman was the first European to discover the islands in the mid seventeenth century and named them New Zealand. British Sea Captain James Cook explored and mapped them between October-March 1769-70. Cook's ship The Endeavour passed close by a French trading ship, the St. Jean–Baptiste, commanded by Captain Jean-Francoise-Marie de Surville off the top of North Island. The ships were sailing in opposite directions and, in the heavy storm, failed to sight each other. The French anchored in one of New Zealand's bays but Captain Surville never set foot on the land. The European missionaries arrived in the early nineteenth century. They were followed by settlers who developed the land and introduced sheep, deer, rabbit and possum. There were wars with the Maori who were never defeated in conflict, only in politics.

We listened to this story while sitting in a beautiful valley. The birds were singing and we were surrounded by strong, tall trees that held huge, soft, silver fern leaves. I felt a tree carving of a Maori chief. He was large, with huge genitalia. I couldn't take my hand away from it – I was fascinated! This caused quite a few laughs from the group. Unfortunately, the invading British destroyed most of these statues, but this one remained, proud and erect!

We had a picnic in a spectacularly scenic clearing; flat, peaceful land everywhere, with the occasional tree or bush. We walked to the river and the waterfall, which had swollen due to the rain; its sound was idyllic. We were in the middle of nowhere and I felt elated. The sense of being in open space was magnificent; I detected the area's energy through my entire body. It was electrifying – a sense that constantly returned to me throughout my travels in New Zealand. We took a short walk along a trail of dry twigs and leaves before returning to Auckland.

I located my new chum from England who I had met earlier at the hostel, and we went into the city centre and found a bar. We had dinner and exchanged stories then moved on to a jazz bar that had live music and returned to the hostel around midnight.

New Zealand beer is inexpensive, although not very strong. A pint cost about $3.50 or $4, which was an excellent price.

I ate well in Auckland, and tried venison and possum for the first time. The New Zealand pies are exceptional; they are available everywhere and are wonderful after a night of drinking! The weather was unhelpful; it rained frequently, which made exploring difficult. I became lost on one walk and discovered a different hostel at the top of the hill in close proximity to where I was staying.

I enquired how to travel around New Zealand, and one of the hostel staff suggested several bus companies. I was told about a travel firm named Kiwi Experience bus tours. For $460 (£150) I could get a bus from Auckland to Christchurch, which stopped in various remote places; I could alight and board whenever I wanted. Accommodation could be organised, activities were available and the ticket lasted for a year. This sounded an excellent idea. New Zealand doesn't have good intercity transportation, and hitchhiking was not recommended as many people take drugs or drink and drive – especially in the countryside.

As I was a Hostel International member (HI) I was able to get a discount, so I booked this ticket, looking forward to the many places I would encounter on my journey south.

Chapter 8

The Kiwi Experience

Whitianga

The first stop on this trip was an east coast town named Whitianga; I booked one night there – which turned into three.

It was around 9th December 2001 when I began my journey on the Kiwi Experience bus. The bad weather followed us and rain precipitated the entire journey. The driver's name was Dee; she was a tough, no-nonsense, dry humoured girl, used to lifting heavy bags and driving large buses. I was given the front passenger seat on a forty-seater coach which was fairly full. She threw my pack in the boot, traversed the city collecting other travellers, and we headed towards our first destination.

The drive to Whitianga took approximately six hours. Dee played music most of the journey and provided information wherever it was appropriate. You can journey around New Zealand in five weeks on the bus, or do it at your leisure, as I did. When the booking form for accommodation was passed down the bus, I said I had already booked a hostel; this was met with a "Nice one, Tony."

On our arrival at the Coromandel Peninsula we turned into the main road and began depositing people. I was dropped off last, along with about five other backpackers. There was one pub and one supermarket in Whitianga.

I met the hostel owner, a big man named Jim, who had a talking parrot that liked to bite. Jim was reasonable, tough and friendly, but a little unsure how to interact with me. I went to the pub and stayed there until closing time.

I spent my other two days exploring Whitianga's small town. I located the supermarket and purchased some food to tie me over until the bus arrived.

Rotorua

Rotorua is a significant Maori area and their culture and traditions play an important roll in the community. The city is situated in the volcanic mountain in the Bay of Plenty region. Because the district's geothermal activity produces sulphur, Rotorua stinks!

The new driver was cool; a large guy and a friendly Maori in his twenties accompanied him. We all joked together, with me saying, "I want some action" and they agreed to find me some!

We drove down the east coast before heading inland. The scenery, once again, was spectacular; breathtaking coastline, beautiful rare birds, giant trees and later rolling hills and mountains. We arrived in Rotorua in mid afternoon. We dropped most of the travellers at their respective hostels, several more at the thermal park, and the three boys and I went to the Agrodome and had some fun! The Agrodome has an associated adventure park where you could bungee jump, go zorbing, participate in a big swing or take a jet boat ride. Three events together cost about $90, (£27). I suggested doing all the events, but the boys said the bungee jump was too small for the likes of me!

Zorbing is an adrenalin sport that was invented by New Zealanders – they like their extreme activities! That is one of the many reasons why I fell in love with New Zealand. You are strapped into a large rubber ball with an inner tyre, and have the option of a wet roll or a dry one – I chose a dry one! Once inside the ball, the door is closed and you are rolled down a big hill. It was fantastic; I wanted to go faster and for longer! I bounced around and went upside down several times, it felt amazing. I followed this with a ride in the jet boat, which was exceptionally fast and I was spun around and got soaked. It only lasted five minutes but really threw me about – a bruising experience. The more pain and thrills there are, the better I like it. I was really crazy back then. I wanted danger, speed and an adrenalin rush; I didn't care!

Finally, the Maori, the large guy and I were put into a body bag suit that zipped up at the back; we were laid out side by side and attached to a big harness and hook, which pulled us off a platform and we swooped over the lake several times. It felt great, an adrenalin rush with the energy sweeping through the length of my body. I was in the middle and stuck my thumbs up; I enjoyed it all.

Afterwards, the guys dropped me at my hostel and said they would collect me later. I introduced myself to the manageress, a friendly, local lady; I asked to stay for five days as I planned to do as much as possible. That night, for $5, we were all invited to a traditional Maori ceremony and meal at Tamaki Village.

The lady showed me to my dorm. The hostel had a bar and restaurant and could cater for about a hundred people. I was given a single room for the same price as a dorm bed. At 6pm, we were organised into groups, piled onto buses and driven to Tamaki Village. Our Maori driver told us what to expect and said we needed a group leader. The young Maori guy I met earlier guided me and the big guy from our bus was designated as our chief.

The Maori greeting is expressed by the rubbing or touching of noses. However, if someone did this three times it was a marriage proposal! Apparently, the Maori Chief would make a formal welcome to which our Chief had to reply appropriately in the Maori language, for us to be accepted. This welcome (powhiri) could, on occasions, be in the form of an aggressive challenge. My

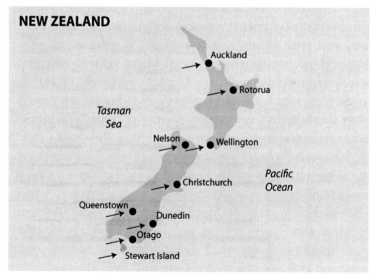

Fig 4: My itinerary in New Zealand

Maori friend told me that the food had been in a *hangi* for hours, a traditional Polynesian cooking method. Food is placed in a shallow hole on stones heated by fire, first meat and then vegetables. Leaves or woven flax covers the hole and food, which cooks slowly over several hours. Fires lit the marae (open meeting place) and I heard Maori instruments being played.

Each group met the Maori chief and the introduction ceremony occurred. We were welcomed, as my big friend said the right words. We entered the wharenui (meeting house), and witnessed a powerful haka performance of song and dance – given by both men and women. I heard the tremendous noise and felt the surge of energy when the final haka was performed. Finally, we had our meal and it was delicious.

We returned to the hostel in time for last orders at the bar. I met the barman; he was a cool guy, a huge Pink Floyd fan, and was dating a lovely Ngati Whakaue girl. The Ngati Whakaue people, the local Maori tribe in Rotorua, were extremely friendly, kind, warm and welcoming like the majority of New Zealanders I met during my travels. New Zealanders were generally quieter than Australians, except when it came to sport – and then they woke up!

I enquired about available excursions. The manageress, who was quite motherly, said I could enjoy a massage and swim at the spa or go white water rafting, which I booked immediately. The lady told me about a Maori cultural tour with a wonderful guide, which sounded interesting, so I arranged a half-day tour for the next morning and went to Hell's Gate and Wai Ora Spa for a mid-afternoon massage.

The hostel had a mini-bus they used to take people to and from the city centre. I was dropped at the Spa and paid $150 (£50) for a mud massage, which was worth every dollar. I splashed around in the thermal pools. There were three or four of them, each increasing in temperature. I tried them all, and relaxed in the water for an hour before my massage. The young lady who met me told me to strip down to my underwear and lie on the bed. She first massaged my body with natural oil, then rubbed mud over my whole body, which was very relaxing. She wrapped me in plastic sheets and left me to sweat for about twenty minutes – the mud and oil opened my pores and removed some of the many toxins from my body. When she returned and unwrapped me, I jumped into a shower that had several hose jets; I removed the mud and then she gave me a second body massage. She was very strong and moved my large fatty muscles – it was exceptional and relaxing. When the hour and a half massage was over, I felt like a new man!

The next morning a huge Maori guy collected me in a 4 × 4 vehicle, and a group of us were driven to Rotowio Marae, the site of a fortified village at the Te Puia Maori Art and Craft Institute. Once there, we formed a circle and all of us made the Maori greeting and said hello: "Tena keo". We explored the courtyard of the Marae where guests are traditionally welcomed and the sacred meeting house, with its carvings and weaved panels, recording the tribes' precious history. The meeting house was a large, wooden building; its roof was made from leaves and grasses. We also visited several boiling sulphur pools – I put my foot on one spot and it was scalding!

The following day I went rafting. I was taken to the Rangitaiki River, approximately half way between Rotorua and Taupo. The young friendly instructor introduced me to the other six members. The river was high due to the heavy rain, but that made for an adventure. Some of the group hadn't rafted before, so we put the raft in the water and practiced the strokes and commands. After we had learnt the basics, we set off. The river was so high that I was being constantly entangled in bushes and hit by tree branches – my helmet was necessary!

We began with small waves until we had gained our confidence, then we tackled the larger rapids. We came through one with a huge splash and I got a lot of water in my face. That particular day was very hot and, again, I got sunburnt. We rafted all day, passing through many tricky rapids. We didn't spill over once, which was excellent – the higher the water, the more dangerous the rapids. We rafted through ten rapids before lunch and another eleven afterwards, and finished with a trio section that included a narrow passage that had large boulders on either side. It was fantastic fun and a great physical experience.

On my final day in the City, I had my all-day bush excursion. A huge Maori, who was about 6 ft 6 in (over 2 metres) in height and must have weighed twenty stone (126 km), collected me in a large amphibious vehicle. I jumped into the back with the others and the adventure began. We performed the greeting ceremony once again. We were informed briefly about the regions natural environment and geothermal activity before going on to a thermal pool at Whakarewarewa Reserve. It was raining and the rocky path, which led to the hot-pool, was slippery. The huge Maori guide picked me up and carried me on his back, which was nuts, as I must have weighed a good 13 stone (88 kg) back then. He took me to the hot pool and just dropped me in like a sack of potatoes.

Following an hour's enjoyment in the hot-pool, we went on an exciting drive through Whirinaki Rainforest. This was a real thrill; I sat on a wheel jack at the back of the small truck. We were bounced up and down, my head hit the roof several times and we were thrown all over the place. The girls sat in the front and hung on. I shouted, loving every minute of it! I felt every bump and turn, and every crash through the undergrowth; I heard tree branches rush past the truck as we pushed our way through. We went deep into the bush and then left the vehicle, and this is where the real challenge began!

Hiking through the forest to our lunch spot along a rough trail, I held on to the guide's backpack, as the space was too narrow to be guided through by linking arms. We stepped over logs and roots, pushed branches aside, and I managed to get several leaves and twigs in my face. Eventually, coming into a clearing, we came upon a bushman's hut. We ducked to get through the entrance and our guide lit the stove and cooked some food; we had tea and ate a good meal.

The second hike was longer and more difficult. I followed the guide down a series of steep steps that were cut into the trail. I felt the guide's drop with my body, staying directly behind and keeping in close contact, sensing for any slight slip or change in step or movement. It was terrific and dangerous. I enjoyed the smell of the soil and forest all around me. The intensity of the enclosed jungle, the darkness of the area plus the coolness provided by the overhead leafy canopy all added to the adventure. I felt everything, noticed the rugged earth steps, felt the vegetation as it snatched at my clothes and scratched my hands and face, smelt the dampness of the approaching river and heard the singing of the birds.

We eventually arrived at the Wiriniki River and walked along the bank using the trees for support. Unfortunately, when I was negotiating a particularly awkward tree that was leaning out towards the river, without any warning, my feet suddenly gave way. The guide was beneath me when I slipped, and he was also forced back and down. I managed to stop my slide by grabbing another tree, but the guide nearly went into the water. I swore a little, laughed and we continued our climb along the bank. I then wrapped my arms around another tree, made a difficult manoeuvre over a root and levered myself up onto firmer ground. The others caught up with us and we continued the trek. The guide decided to leave me in a particular spot and return with the truck. I wanted to continue the hike, as I didn't worry about danger, but he said it was far too difficult, even for me.

I went to sleep under a tree in the silent rainforest.

Some time later, I heard the group cross the Whirinaki River and the guide return. He could not find me and kept calling my name. I lay in wait and, as he approached, I shouted out and scared the shit out of him! He swore a couple of times in surprise and then we both had a laugh about it. After collecting everybody, we began the long, bumpy journey back. Everyone was tired and thirsty;

I had cut my hands, elbows and feet, and had damaged my flip-flops. The return drive through the rainforest was fun. We climbed a few hills, and bushes whacked me as my window was open. It felt great – I was face to face with the real environment and I enjoyed it all. The atmosphere smelled damp; a natural aroma that cannot be described, but anyone who has been in similar terrain will understand. It is the smell of soil after the rain has fallen, fresh and natural.

Waitomo

Waitomo is a small town slightly to the east of Rotorua. We arrived around 2 pm; the hostel was quiet and there were few guests. I wanted to explore the caves, my main reason for visiting Waitomo. There were many activities available – canoeing, horse riding, jet boat driving and all manner of caving and black water rafting trips. One adventure included jumping rivers, rock climbing, abseiling, swimming and hiking. I assessed my options and settled for a three-hour black water tubing experience.

After a breakfast in a café opposite the hostel, I was collected for my tour. I had my own guide, who was a powerfully built lady. I was kitted out with a wet suit, rubber footwear and a helmet. The water in the caves was 10–14 degrees Celsius. The small group consisted of six people. The idea of black water tubing is to sit in a rubber ring, similar to a car tyre, and move oneself down the cavernous river. We walked to the caves, dragging our rafting rings behind us, stepping over a series of rocks and boulders, which I found tiresome. We entered our first cave and it became dark, at least for everyone else!

Water covered my feet but it was shallow. I climbed up rough, rock steps and across boulders to get to the larger caves; it was an enjoyable challenge.

We came upon a large waterfall where we had to climb up on a rock shelf and then down again to get past it. We found deeper water further into the cave; I floated my ring, sat in it and let the current carry me downstream. I passed through two large caves where the echoes were loud and deep. I tested the water temperature with my hand – it was freezing! After what seemed like only minutes, but was obviously much longer, I reached the end of the large cave and was back in shallow water. I climbed out of the ring and, with help, clambered up the rock face and back onto dry land.

Afterwards, I was driven to the lake to drive a jet boat. I was given a life jacket and helmet. The only instruction I received was to keep my foot on the accelerator! The challenge was to drive the boat around an obstacle course shaped like a figure of eight. I put my foot on the accelerator pedal and, with my instructor beside me, placed my hands on the wheel. He covered my hands with his, started the ignition and we blasted off. At first, he tried telling me when to turn, but I was unable to hear him so he helped with the steering. We went really fast, about 40 miles per hour (or 60 kilometres per hour) which was fantastic. I felt the power surge through me and the spray went everywhere. We spun the wheel and nearly ran over a course object – it was thrilling, I was in charge of a fast, electrifying machine and too soon that ride, which was way too short, was over.

The following morning I went to some stables and

a lovely girl took me horse riding for an hour along Waitomo's hilly trails. I was on one horse and she rode in front. It was very peaceful, I enjoyed the ride and the girl was great company. Horses are lovely animals, strong and loyal. Afterwards, I went to the café near the hostel to wait for the bus to arrive.

Taupo

The town of Taupo lies on the shore of Lake Taupo – New Zealand's largest lake in surface area. The region is both mountainous and volcanic. We arrived in the town as night was falling. The female manager at the Taupo HI was a rather rude woman in her mid-forties. She demanded to see everybody's passports, a document I hadn't used for weeks.

After taking my details, she showed me to my dorm, which was accessed by a set of metal stairs. It was an old building with a large reception area, but no kitchen or lounge. The hostel was unstaffed after 8 pm. I found it to be a poor hostel, and must say I wouldn't recommend it to other travellers.

After visiting the reception, I learnt that Taupo has many activities. These include skydiving, bungee jumping, nature and mountain walks. There is also a plethora of water sports, including fishing, kayaking, water-skiing and sailing. Sadly, it rained almost continuously during my two days in Taupo and, because my hearing aids react badly to water, I was unable to participate in any of the water-based activities.

Eventually, I caught the Kiwi Experience bus to the next destination.

Taihape

Our driver was another cool guy, young and good fun. I got to know him as we travelled through the countryside. We listened to music and bumped along at a terrific speed. It took all day to get to the isolated farming town of Taihape, which is a secluded place with hills, valleys and a small river. We pulled up at the River Valley Adventure Lodge around 4 pm, and everyone walked down a steep, muddy hill to reach the lodge. The bags and I were loaded into a jeep and driven down in style! The manageress made us feel very welcome, described the surrounding area, explained about available activities and informed everyone where they were sleeping. Dinner was available and you put your name on a list – I tried to include my name twice!

I was shown to an upstairs three-bedroom dorm. The toilet was outside, but I just peed in the bushes when necessity called. It was an unusual place – I was greeted by drilling and banging when I entered the reception area – it was a building site!

On the journey to Taihape, an activity list had been handed round; there was a bungee jump, a horse ride or a walk to choose from. Our group numbered about twenty, and the bus wasn't full; they rarely had been on the northern leg. I included my name for the bungee jump, as it was a big one – 240 ft (80 metres). Now that sounded adventurous! The evening flowed by gently, very relaxing. There was a wood fire to keep us all warm, along with beer and young women – I was in my element!

After breakfast, the manager of the lodge drove me to Kokai Gravity Canyon on the Rangitikei River for my bridge bungee. There was a wooden shed-like building where the bungee jump was organised and I met the instructors. It was a damp, chilly morning, but there was no wind. I paid about $100, and they explained what would happen.

They weighed me, to get the length of the bungee cord correct, and then strapped my ankles together using a towel for padding. They said, "We'll take you to the edge of the platform and after three taps on the shoulder, you jump off." They told me to raise my arms above my head and just fall forward.

Apart from the hostel manager watching, and the three instructors, I was all alone. My adrenalin was flowing and I couldn't wait to start. The bungee cord was attached to my ankle strap and I was taken to the edge by shuffling forward. I felt more like a trussed up chicken as I hopped rather than walked. I was on the platform edge and my toes could feel air. I removed my hearing aids, something I did before most physical activities, and they tapped me three times; without any hesitation, I fell forwards and dropped into the air!

I had a two or three seconds freefall… then bang! The bungee cord stretched out, then recoiled – and I bounced! It was like being smacked into a brick wall, my whole body was jerked upright. I almost became entangled in the rope and then I was spun around in the air. I bounced again – it was a jolt each time, and I didn't know when it would happen; I had no anticipation and this is what made it even more fantastic. It was an unpredicted explosion, my entire body felt the impact with air and the bounce of recoil. Electric waves of energy and adrenalin passed through me. Not knowing what would occur next was exulting and fantastic; the danger, the fear, the madness – I loved it all and wanted more.

After the third or fourth bounce, the rope slackened and I was upside-down and swinging. The pull began on my ankles, which hurt.

It suddenly occurred to me as I was hanging upside-down, they hadn't told me how I was to get back up. I thought, how do I return to the top? Then I realised I was being lowered. After swinging for a while, I was caught by another instructor and pulled to the ground. I had my ankles untied and, after shouting and swearing, "Shit... wahoo... that was fuckin' great, thanks!" I was led up lots of steps back to the top where the others met me. They all shook my hand and I was given a certificate. We jumped into the jeep and returned to the lodge – I was ecstatic.

There was a small bottle of beer on the front seat and I took it, removed the cap with my teeth and knocked it back. The driver put on some AC/DC, I turned up the volume, and we rocked all the way back. In the afternoon, we all piled back onto the bus and went to Wellington at the bottom of North Island.

Most people that use the Kiwi Experience bus go to stay one night in Wellington and continue on the bus the next day. However, I wished to explore New Zealand's capital city. It was almost Christmas and I had plenty of time. I had to organise my $40 ferry ticket and arrange a day to be collected.

I knew it would be difficult to get accommodation anywhere around that time, so I booked five days in

Wellington initially, but on realising I was only staying one night in River Valley, I rearranged my stay.

Wellington
On arrival in Wellington, I was dropped at the HI, a large place that was almost empty. Again, I had walked into a building site, as they were constructing extensions to the hostel. The building resembled a hotel.

The staff, who were mostly female, helped me with directions and allowed me to stay for an extra week, even though this was against normal policy. I quickly discovered that Wellington had some tourist attractions. There was the enticing harbour and the huge Maori historical and cultural museum spread over five floors. Also, there were several interesting coastal walks and the naval museum. However, once I had investigated all these places, then the city's other main activity was drinking!

My location was fantastic; the hostel was just around the corner from Princes Street, the main thoroughfare, which had about twenty Irish pubs and local bars. Opposite the hostel was a large supermarket where I could buy food and beer, so I stocked up immediately. Finally, on the other side of the square was a brothel, which I discovered later. I went to the large Maori museum, which is only a ten-minute walk from the hostel.

One of the receptionists, a tall, long-haired, attractive young lady became my acquaintance. She took me across to the museum after checking to see if guides were available. I had an hour's tour and the guide described some artefacts that were on display, including a Waka (war canoe). I entered a replica of a Maori camp, where there were pots, cooking utensils and weapons similar to those I had felt in Australia. There were also stuffed animals and some painted eggs including one from a Kiwi bird. A Kiwi is a non-flying native bird that forages on the ground.

I visited the small navel museum on the waterfront, which contained a history of Wellington's navigation, charting the old stories of the ferries from North Island to South Island. Wellington's harbour is sizable, enabling the British battleship HMS Hood to pay a visit during her 1922 world cruise; a plaque hangs in the museum marking the occasion. The harbour is subject to fierce winds that emanate from the Antarctic – believe me, it is a windy city! The Cook Strait divides North and South Islands and is a very choppy channel at the best of times. In 1962, there was a harbour disaster, when a fierce storm caused the sinking of a ferry with all lives lost. I finished my day with an exploration of New Zealand's Houses of Parliament.

I took a bus to the north of the city and joined a group of tourists for an hour's free guided tour around New Zealand's political headquarters. We visited the three main buildings of the parliamentary complex.; Parliament House, with its debating chamber, Executive Wing (Beehive), and the Parliamentary Library, which is the oldest of the three buildings. The Executive Wing houses the government and the Prime Minister's Office. The building is called the "Beehive" because of its shape. We were informed that New Zealand's Prime Minister was a woman and she was only the second female to hold that office – she had been there since late 1999.

In Parliament House, we were permitted to enter the debating chamber where Parliament (House of Representatives) conducts political debate. It was organised like the British parliament, with some slight differences. Elections occur every three years and the Parliament is unicameral – there is no Upper House. Queen Elizabeth II, New Zealand's Head of State, opened the completed new Parliament House in 1995. The half-finished building had been used since 1918. The original parliament buildings, excluding the library, were destroyed in a fire in 1907.

The entrance hall was large and polished, and at the foot of the enormous staircase that led to the debating chamber was a statue of an Indian elephant that was a gift from the King of Thailand, on his visit in the late 1950s. It always faced east as a sign of good luck, so I touched the large elephant on my exit.

Once back in the city centre I found a large Irish pub, which not only served Guinness, but also had live music and Irish food. I had a stew and began a heavy drinking session that lasted for two months! The beer was cheap, although Guinness was a similar price to that in England. I danced to the band until the pub closed around 3 am. I frequented this pub most nights after I discovered its close proximity to the hostel.

One afternoon I had a harbour tour that cost around $9 and lasted for about two hours. A commentary was given aboard the uncovered speedboat. It went really fast; I got wet several times, but that only added to the fun!

Later, I returned to the centre and had a meal in a quiet pub before going in search of more lively entertainment.

On Christmas Eve, I stocked the hostel fridge with beer and went to the pub. A band was playing until midnight and, unfortunately I managed to knock over their Christmas tree.

I spent most of Christmas Day relaxing in the hostel and talking to various people. The city was deserted. I met an English couple who were travelling, and an interesting gentleman in his late forties who was wandering around the world. He had to telephone his daughter who lived in Japan. He took me to the cricket ground on Boxing Day to watch New Zealand thrash Bangladesh – there was no contest! I sat on the hill in the sun; the game didn't start until midday. The weather intervened late in the afternoon to make the game interesting, and it lasted three days. If not for the weather, the game might not have lasted past two days.

On Boxing Day night, I got really drunk in the Irish bar and left around 1 am. To get to the hostel, I had to take a couple of subtle turns. I withdrew some money from the cash machine – I just pressed buttons until I got money. It was a simple machine; most are far more complex. I managed to walk past the hostel and again, got myself lost. I suddenly heard some music. I followed the sound and discovered a building, which I entered and found myself in a store room. I continued to walk towards the sound of the music until I came upon what I thought was a party. A young lady approached me in a sexy dress and smelling of nice fragrance saying, "Hi, honey."

I asked where I was and said I was trying to find the hostel.

She said, "I know where you want to go." She then said,

"This is a brothel!" and told me it cost $200 for an hour.

I searched my wallet, knowing I only had $150 on me. She said that would be enough for twenty minutes, so I thought, why not? It's Christmas!

After my moment of pleasure, she walked me to the hostel and I kissed her before entering. What a night that was. New Year's Eve was a similar blast; I went to the Irish bar early and got paralytic again. I danced to the two bands, met a lovely young Scottish girl, some Irish ladies and rolled home about 5 am.

I spent the next day, 1st January 2002, walking around the harbour in the cool breeze, enjoying the tranquillity of Wellington's portside. The following morning, I took a local bus to the harbour, where I joined the other members of the Kiwi Experience bus for the ride to South Island and the next adventure.

Chapter 9

New Zealand: Wild and Dangerous

South Island
On the morning of 2nd January 2002, I crossed the Cook Strait by ferry and journeyed to Nelson, the first major town and a three-hour drive from the port. I had arranged a hostel from Wellington and was expected for three nights.

Nelson
The small hostel had friendly staff. It was close to a supermarket and near the city centre. I enquired about activities and was told I could go sky diving, which I considered, or sea kayaking, which also appealed. There was a wine tour, which I booked for the next day before arranging the kayaking. Nelson is a small and pleasant town on the northwest coast, named after the British admiral of the late eighteenth/early nineteenth centuries. There are many good bars on the main street, which was only a ten-minute walk from the hostel.

I was collected by an amiable guy and, along with twelve other people, went wine tasting. Once we had travelled inland, the scenery became green and lush; there were mountains and valleys and the fresh country air was delicious; the warmth of the sun only added to the day's quality. We stopped for our first wine taste just after 10 am. There were several wines available, all different flavours and ages. The sweeter the wine, the more I enjoyed it. Our guide, a wine connoisseur, said, "We should take a glass of wine, have a sip and hold the liquid in our mouths and let it flow over our tongues and run to the back of the throat." He said to swill it around my mouth before swallowing because this would enhance the wine's flavour on my taste buds and improve the enjoyment.

I tried this and it felt strange, but delightful. It was an odd sensation, the liquid felt smooth and cool, slightly sharp, but also rich. I tasted the four wines presented, and I particularly liked two, but rejected one completely.

We continued to another vineyard and repeated the wine tasting technique. We visited about four wineries before we had lunch in a picturesque village. One of the wineries produced Port and once I had sampled that, there was no stopping me – I was hooked. Everyone on the trip was becoming more relaxed. We eventually made a slow retreat back to Nelson after a pleasant day.

The next morning I was taken to the beach in the bay to go sea kayaking, even though the weather was overcast and a storm was threatened. I met the guide, a friendly, young, fresh-faced guy and was given a wetsuit and lifejacket and introduced to the group. There was a lovely Irish girl, who was paired with me to begin with, a Dutch couple and a Japanese guy. I had kayaked before, so knew how to use the double bladed paddle; it had alternating ends that were at opposite angles to each other. You put one end in the water, pull back, then lift that end out of the water, roll your wrists and plunge the other end in, repeating this at regular intervals and creating a rhythm; you paddle in the opposite direction to go backwards. A single blade is used for turning the kayak. We were shown how to operate the crafts while we were on the beach. We wore a canvas cover to keep us dry when we were paddling.

A kayak is long, narrow and pointed, in order to provide swift movement through the water. There are single, two or three person crafts; we used two person kayaks. Just as we were about to start, a terrific storm broke and we had to take cover. When the rain eased, the guide asked us if we still wanted to go. The consensus was, "Yes, let's get kayaking!"

We pulled our kayaks into the sea, climbed in and pushed off. I paddled madly and made good progress. The current took over and paddling was easy. The sea enveloped me; it felt like I was sitting right in it. Each time I put a blade in the water, my arms became wet and dripped onto my cover. My fingers became sore and blistered from paddling but the activity was enjoyable. We travelled mostly along the picturesque coast, staying near to the shore. I had brought sun cream, a bottle of water and a hat: essential items for this type of trip. It was an all-day adventure and we made great progress to each destination, although we failed to spot any sea creatures. There were many sea birds; I heard the gulls cry and the guide told me about other birds that were diving for food or sitting amongst the rocks.

The first bay we stopped in was shallow. When we

neared shore our guide powered me onto the beach. The sea was strong and terrific – most enjoyable. I was immensely happy to be on the water, to hear and feel its powerful surge. After a rest on the sandy beach, we headed off to our next destination, a large bay where we would stop for lunch, a good two-hour's paddling.

We kayaked in formation. I put my back into it, using my large shoulders to do most of the work, and soon had a steady rhythm. We reached the destination ahead of time and had a well-earned rest. The bay was large and scattered with rocks. Seagulls flew overhead, crying and searching for fish. Large cliffs stood behind us pronouncing the headland. We were a good distance away from Nelson, out in the elements and felt privileged to have such a glimpse of nature.

We relaxed for a good hour and finally set off on the long journey home. I was determined to be the first back, and I succeeded, after much paddling and grunting; the others arrived close behind. I was exhausted – my body was sore all over, my face and arms were sunburnt, but I didn't care as I was having fun doing an activity that I never would have dreamed possible in England.

The next morning I met a group from the Kiwi Experience bus and we tackled the beautiful, wild, west coast. The destination was Westport, a small isolated town. First, however, there were some further activities on offer. There were two choices – sea kayaking or a hike through Kaiteriteri National Park – I chose the hike. Two girls were also going, one from England named Hannah, and another from Spain. We had a forty minute drive from Nelson before the two girls and I were dropped at a small harbour where we caught a speedboat to the National Park.

The boat was packed; I boarded at the back, climbing up a small ladder. I was wearing my flip-flops, inappropriate hiking footwear. After a twenty-minute ride, we were deposited close to the beach. We waded through the shallows onto the sand and then passed through a gate that led onto the trail. We had about two and a half hours there, although we took around three hours and nearly missed the boat back. It was fantastic; I was out in the natural environment with two beauties. We swapped travel stories as we walked. The weather kept fluctuating between drizzle and warm sun, so we were continuously putting on and removing our rain jackets. The trail undulated, though it was mostly a soft turf path that snaked through forest and bush land. It ran parallel to the shore and we climbed for several minutes getting high above the sea level. I was able to smell the sea air, and at intervals, heard the surf crashing against the rocks far below. We regularly came across small square drain ditches that we had to step over. I almost twisted my ankle on one; they were extremely annoying, if not very dangerous.

We hiked along, ascending and descending, stepping over ditches, tree roots and generally having fun. It was a challenge for me, as I'm not very fit. There was little room on the path and we were being careful. When I fell, naturally I released my grip on the girl who was guiding me, and went down the bank. While I was attempting to manoeuvre around a tree that was leaning out obscurely towards the drop, I slipped and fell. We were high up on a cliff edge, where we had walked for a good time. A high vertical rock wall was on our left and a sheer drop of a grass bank on the right. I managed to drop my cane and left it on the path. I grabbed onto the long grass and this stopped my fall from being anything more than just a short slide down the cliff.

I swore, and after catching my breath – and my balance – I began to climb back up onto the path. I was able to get to the top and crawled over the edge with help from the two girls. As I was climbing back up, one of my flip-flops fell off, but luckily was caught in the grass. A couple passing the other way saw what had happened and came to help. They used my cane, which had a hook on the top of it, to fish my flip-flop back for me. I thanked them for their efforts, and after a moment's pause to rest from the shock, we continued our walk.

Towards the end of the hike, we came across a series of steps cut into the trail; many were rugged and disfigured. One girl went in front of me and the other followed behind. The girl in front guided me down each step, I put one hand on her shoulder, which enabled me to feel her descent. Finally, though late, we arrived at the end of the trail. All we had to do was run across the beach into the water and rejoin the speedboat that whisked us back across the bay where we boarded the bus.

Westport

We arrived in Westport as evening fell; it was dark as hell and raining hard. The hostel I stayed at was homely; the owner was friendly and helpful. He welcomed me and took me to my dorm, which was like a self-contained cottage. There was a kitchen, bathroom and two bedrooms. I was the only occupant. The reception was separate from the dorm house. His son, a twenty year old, worked with him and was just as friendly. The floor was uncarpeted because they had just had a flood. Summer in New Zealand means rain.

I took an overland tour with a large, happy New Zealander in an amphibious vehicle. As we drove down a rough track, he described to me the expansive grassy terrain that mostly grazed deer and sheep. It was very quiet except for the vehicle's engine, and I could smell the freshness of the countryside through my open window – sweet, clean, summer air and newly cut grass. We spotted several deer and horses in the fields as they ran from our noise. The sheep, however, didn't move. We eventually drove into a field where my guide alighted and opened a farm gate. We set off across the boggy ground; it was so peaceful, we hardly met a soul all day. I felt every bump and jolt, as the big 4 × 4 vehicle bounced across the rough terrain. We discussed a variety of subjects including deer breeding, which is carried out on large farms in New Zealand. Our guide could not believe I was travelling around the world alone blind; I said it was great and a fantastic way to meet people. He loved my open-minded attitude, and explained to me how the vehicle had normal and four-wheel drive, the latter for harsh terrain like wet ground or sand. We backed up, ready to jump a river. However, so much of the bank had been washed away, that he could not see its depth. We failed to reach the other side, and because of our weight, the front wheels went into the mud and we were stuck, with our back wheels spinning. We hit the mud heavily, tipping the vehicle at such an angle as to prevent me from climbing out. The guide said he had a winch on the front, and attached it to a tree, but when he tried to winch the truck out, the tree shot out of the ground like a missile! After two failed attempts, he said he would go and find help. About an hour later, the guide and a farmer returned with a tractor, and we were pulled clear and were able to resume our tour.

Some time later, we pulled into a farmyard and were greeted by three large, friendly dogs. We briefly chatted with the farmer and his wife and then continued our tour. We finished at a place near the coast; I could smell the sea air. Due to the accident with the vehicle in the river, we arrived late at our rendezvous for dinner. After the meal we returned to Westport.

The following day I boarded the Kiwi Experience bus for the next adventure. The new driver's name was Cain; he gave me a front seat and I recognised immediately upon boarding that the passengers were a good crowd, as the jokes began flying. Cain and Able and much more! I told them I would drive, which received a positive response. I was my usual charismatic self, announcing that the music was shit and that New Zealanders have odd shaped balls! There were two buses and we raced each other when the highway was clear. When a rival company passed by, we made lots of noise, Cain beeped the horn and we shouted rude words! I met some of the gang that became my mates for the trip, as far as Queenstown at least. There were a couple of guys behind me named Paul and Dave. There was also another guy named Paul, who was much taller.

Paul one was small and from Manchester. There was a Scottish girl named Kirsty, and not forgetting Deanna from Canada. She was delicious and I grew to fancy her; she was noisy, and one of the lads.

Mahinapua to Wanaka

The bus was overcrowded, and we were overloaded with luggage. Once my backpack was swung aboard, I didn't find it again until I arrived in Queenstown. We drove to Mahinapua, in the middle of the New Zealand wilderness. A man in his early eighties owned the Mahinapua Hotel (the legendary Poo Pub). Payment was in cash and finding a bed was a lottery. Cain said, "What can we do with Tony? I know, let's put him in the bar."

Hence, my reputation began. The barmaid introduced herself, and I asked for a large beer. I was in South Island now, so it was Spate beer, which was stronger than Red Lion. The hostel was equipped with a dance floor, a restaurant and a kitchen, where I included my name for dinner. Cain showed me to a dorm, he said it didn't really matter where I ended up! There were plants and bushes everywhere, the toilet was outside and I knew what that meant – in the bushes, Tony! We were near a lake and, apparently, gloworms and frogs could be easily spotted. Some of the gang went down to the lake, while I drank more beer; they even made their own home brew that was over eight percent proof, which almost blew my head off! Some time during the evening, dinner was served and I chatted to one of the guys who showed me where we could find some women's clothes for the forthcoming party. Guys were meant to dress up as women, and girls as sexy tarts in black bin liners; it was all a laugh. One of the guys found me a little dress, but it only came down to my buttocks! I asked a German girl to lend me some underwear; she volunteered a bra, but refused any panties! I was undecided what to do with my boxer shorts that were showing under the short dress, so I thought, sod it, and removed them. I entered the party wearing no underwear, apart from the black lacy bra! Apparently I looked really sexy?! I walked around hugging people and chatted up some of the girls. The party lasted until dawn. I was told not to sit down as my penis showed. I crashed around 4 am, only to be woken up by Cain, who said it was time to go.

I dressed, removed the bra I had slept in, and boarded the bus to our next adventure. Most of the group were hung over, but I was feeling fine. We had breakfast then I went for a tour at the Bushman's Centre. I encouraged Paul one, who was still wearing make up from the previous night, to join me. The tour guide was a rough talking bushman, and he laughed at the sight of Paul and I together.

He began the tour by talking about possums, and held one up by its tail. When I went to stand beside him he said, "This one is a little sad because he has just seen his mate killed on the slab!" The girls groaned at that.

He gave the possum to me, "Here Tony, this is the tail. Those sharp bits are its teeth!" Everyone laughed.

I lifted the possum up and down by its tail, and said, "Bungee jump possum" and half the group cracked up.

Next, we looked at an eel, which he pulled out of a small pond.

He said, "Tony, touch this... What does it feel like?" I smiled and said, "It feels like a vagina!"

He almost dropped the eel as he was in hysterics; most of the group were wetting themselves by this point. He looked at Paul one and said, "Where have you been taking Tony?"

Paul just smiled. After that, the guide introduced a bush pig to us. He said it was a wild, dangerous, dirty animal and kicked it up the ass. I asked if I could touch it and he said, "Your life in your own hands!"

We went and played with some of the bushman's weapons; he showed us how to throw a knife and axe. He said, "Don't throw them the wrong way Tony." I asked,

"Why has it gone quiet?"

He replied, "They've all sneaked away quietly!"

I threw both weapons, but they didn't stick in the target. When I threw the axe, it rebounded off the wall. I fired a bow and arrow and almost hit the bull's eye. Finally, I was given the chance to fire a paint ball pistol.

The guide said, "I want to tell you to look down the barrel Tony."

I said, "You first." I took the gun in both hands, had it lined up, pulled the trigger and hit the target.

We drove to Franz Josef nestled in the Westland National Park. The HI where I resided was relaxing, though it was quite a distance from where the others were staying. We spent two days in the village; the group hiked Franz Josef Glacier, while I had a heli-hike to the top of the ice mountain. The helicopter ride was expensive, but this was the only way I could experience the glacier. The chopper was noisy, but once on the ice field after a fifteen-minute ride, it was heavenly. The cold, hard snow under my feet was crunchy and fascinating – the space was immense.

On the way to Wanaka, we visited Puzzling World in the morning and had a paintball war game in the afternoon.

At Puzzling World someone bet $60 for me to be the first out of the maze. I said, "Put your money away, you daft bugger."

Deanna offered to go round the maze with me. I said, "We have a problem, it says you need common sense and good sight to negotiate a maze, and I'm blind and you're North American!"

We did attempt it, but failed. I also went on a golf range where I had to hit balls as far as possible. Cain lined me up and I whacked them. I did reasonably well, until I hit one the wrong way and everybody stopped their activities as they were in hysterics. I asked to fire a gun, so Cain took me to the shooting gallery, where the man showed me a twelve-bore rifle. He told me how to load and fire the weapon, pressed a pedal releasing a disc, and I fired both barrels, but missed. The explosion of the rifle and the recoil against my shoulder was powerful and left me feeling slightly bruised and deafened.

After that, I fired a twenty-two-calibre rifle. This weapon was on a stand and I had seven shots. Again, the instructor showed me how to load the gun; he lined me up and I fired. I put my first shot clean through the bull's eye and my other shots were in the twenty-five ring, either side of the bull. The guys were astonished when I showed them my targets.

During the bus journey we stopped for a paintball war game. The area swarmed with sand flies and the bastards were everywhere; they descended upon me like rain or fleas on a dog. We were given overalls and helmets with visors to cover our face. The guns were long barrelled and held fifty small paintballs ready to fire. We were in a wooded area and I stood behind a thick clump of trees, as this afforded me some protection. The remainder of the group began a running battle; I fired my gun at any sound, but didn't hit much in the first battle. We were told that when the whistle sounded the game was over. In the second round, I joined a group behind a wooden barricade. I hid and fired my weapon through a hole, spraying an area where I thought the other group might run through. I managed to hit one girl twice. Her shrieks were hilarious. Someone shot me in the thumb and in the back during the third and last game; it hurt when it hit your flesh, so a paintball in the face could be quite nasty.

I spent a quiet night in the lake-town Wanaka, relaxing before my sky dive the following morning.

On the morning of my sky dive Cain took four of us to a small airstrip. A big guy took care of me; we were kitted up, then sat on the aeroplane's outer door and practiced the dive and roll positions. We took off in the small plane and climbed to 15,000 ft (5,000 metres). Once we levelled out at the correct height, I was attached to my partner and the door was opened; we had a quick safety check and I was dragged to the opening. My heart was thumping and I was perspiring profusely. I sat on the edge and on three taps, after crossing my arms, my companion propelled me forwards out of the plane and into the beautiful morning sky. We rolled over several times, caught by the plane's turbulence and spun around. We levelled out in a horizontal position. I steadied my breathing and enjoyed the freefall. It was like surfing, but on air instead of on water. The fierce wind snapped at my face and the hot sun warmed the air. The sensation of sky diving was like riding on a large bubble. I was pushed around by the wind's strong current whilst simultaneously being dragged towards earth by the forces of gravity and our combined weights. I sweated inside my jumpsuit and this trickled down my body. I felt soaked to the skin and itchy all over.

Roughly sixty seconds later, my partner pulled the parachute cords and the pain of the harness digging into my legs began. The fire of agony surged through my muscles momentarily before I adjusted the straps and relaxed. The day was lovely, and I felt the sun's heat as we swooped around the sky, and floated over alpine lakes and the stunning Mount Aspiration National Park rain forest. My partner tapped me and this was the signal to lift up my legs. I did, and we came into land on a field, with a bump and a slide to the side. We were down.

My guide cut the parachute chords and we were on terra firma again. He shook my hand, "Great one, Tony. How do you feel?"

"Bloody great!" I replied.

We waited for the others to land, all shook hands, and rejoined the group.

Chapter 10

New Zealand:
Queenstown and the south end of the country

Queenstown: Part One

Queenstown is an international resort in the Otago region on the south-west coast of South Island. It is built around Queenstown Bay inlet on the glacial carved Lake Wakatitu. The town's exterior contains large rocky areas connected to mountain peaks, bisected by rivers and roads. The diverse terrain contains everything from deep ravines and rolling hills to steep valleys and rugged mountains. Milford Sound and the Pacific Ocean are just on the town's doorstep, which add to the beauty of the area.

During the journey through the Otago Region, a form was passed around the bus, and I added my name for the world famous AJ Hackett Kawarau Bridge bungee. Cain told us that when we arrived we should go to the Experience Shop to arrange any activities. We stopped near the bridge on the outskirts of Queenstown and everyone alighted. About half the group planned to try the bungee. I was weighed and asked for a video and pictures. You jump from the bridge and pay later!

There are numerous stories about bungee jumping. Arguably it originated as an ancient ritual on Pentecost Island, Vanuatu, in the South Pacific. Bungee jumping as a commercial sport began in New Zealand in the late 1980s.

I weighed in for that first jump at 189.2 lbs (86 kg), which was written on my arm. One of the AJ Hackett crew walked me to the bridge where I climbed some steps to the platform. There was music playing and the remainder of the group were watching me and cheering. Paul one agreed to wait for me at the bottom and walk me back to the top. I was told that I would be lowered into a boat and they would touch me with a pole. They strapped my ankles together, attached the bungee cord and took me to the edge. I smiled at the camera and said something rude. After three taps on my back, I jumped. I heard a big cheer, and then I was gone.

I jumped with my legs going forward, almost hitting my head on the platform and ended up falling down backwards until the rope caught my fall, pulled me up, and I bounced. I shouted my lungs out, loving the shock and the sensation. Two more bounces and then I hung upside down, suspended in mid-air on the end of a large rubber condom! That is how I would describe it. I slowly descended to the water, until suddenly, without any warning, I was hit on the head by a pole. I grabbed it and was pulled into the raft, untied and taken to the shore. I was given my hearing aids, my footwear and my cane and then Paul one and I climbed back up the hill. At the top, I was given a hero's welcome. Deanna went next and you could hear her screams, followed by big Paul and several others.

Afterwards, Cain and I went to the Kiwi Experience Centre to meet some of the female staff and to book my week's itinerary. Cain was in Queenstown for four days before he returned north. My plan was to visit Stewart Island, and Cain mentioned a Bottom Bus for only $150 (£50) that would take me around the bottom half of the country, enabling me to travel to Stewart Island.

I signed up for two more bungee jumps, and paid for the three jumps together, which gave me a discount. I also paid for a day trip to Milford Sound, before asking about other available activities. There are many events and adventures in Queenstown and it is changing and improving constantly. Skydiving, light plane aerobatics, various rafting trips, jet boat rides, plus a four-event option were all available. The awesome foursome sounded attractive. After booking everything possible, Cain and I went to see one of his friends about riding a motorbike. The guy was huge and after hearing what events I had already booked, he said he'd be delighted to take me. I said I wanted two wheels and he agreed.

Cain dropped me at the HI, and had told everyone earlier that we were to meet at a certain pub around 8 pm, where the party would commence. The HI was at the far end of town and quite a distance from the action.

A friendly receptionist greeted me. I asked to stay five days if possible and he said that was fine, but I might have to change rooms. He showed me up two separate flights of stairs and along a carpeted corridor to my dorm.

At the pub, Cain immediately bought me a large beer. We had all been given tokens that allowed us two drinks for the price of one. The gang arrived in small groups, but soon most of them were there, and the atmosphere was great. The small, noisy pub had a square bar and an outside seating area. Cain introduced me to a couple named Andy and Sally, who ran a river boarding company. They were really friendly, like almost every New Zealander I had met. Someone grabbed me and said, "Come on, Tony. We're off to the World Bar." I just followed.

The World Bar resembled a nightclub with loud music and a lively atmosphere. There were large teapots containing different types of vodka. I was given small shots; I didn't know what they were, but I still drank them. People just gave them to me and I must have had about ten by the time we left. The World Bar closed at 3 am and although I was moaning that I wanted to go to another pub, I was bundled into a taxi and dropped at the HI – somehow I managed to get to my dorm.

I spent the majority of my time in Queenstown's centre. I liked it there, with its numerous bars, man-made lake, and a main street which branches off and leads to the many independent hostels. The atmosphere was pulsating and the area's natural energy crackled – it was tremendous.

The next afternoon Cain collected me for my motorbike ride. At the bike shed I had to complete a health and safety form. The owner gave me overalls and a helmet and said he would only charge me half price, as I could not see the scenery! I rode with the owner while Cain and another guy rode separately. My bike was a large 450 cc. I climbed on, placed my arms around the big man, put my feet on two protruding pegs and we set off. The machine pulsated under my body and I felt every jolt and vibration.

Once you leave any town on south island, except perhaps Christchurch, you're in isolated terrain. We left the town and rode up one of the mountains, through a forest, doing jumps and wheelies. He asked me if I was okay, and I said, "Yes, no worries, it's great."

I had to hold on tight, as my feet kept coming off the pegs because of the machine's force. We reached a good 70 miles per hour (100 kilometres per hour). The jumps were fantastic. I hugged my body close to my driver and dropped down as we jumped, rising up again as we landed. Going through the forest, the trees were so close that I got branches in my face and leaves in my mouth. At one point, I was almost strangled and pulled off the bike by a branch that became wrapped around my neck. I just held on and the force of the bike pulled me through. We twisted our way up the mountain climb, going so steep at one point that I swear I thought we would tip over. However, my driver knew his business and handled the machine skilfully.

At the top, we stopped for a rest on a plateau, so I quickly removed my helmet and gloves and wiped sweat from my head; it was hot in that gear. Cain asked me how I was doing; I smiled and said, "Fine. It's bloody great."

We had a fifteen-minute rest, some water was passed around and we climbed back onto the bikes. We rode around the plateau, over grass bumps and down hollows, before starting the descent to Queenstown. The ride down the mountain was breathtaking. We flew down the steep gradient and I hung on for dear life. Descending the mountain was more difficult. Natural gravity caused me to slide forwards on top of my driver. I tried to stand up more on the footplates, and keep my weight off him, but it was difficult to judge when we descended a gradient and when we levelled out. Then suddenly, it was over; we pulled into the bike shop. I dumped the gear and we all went for a beer.

In the evening, a young lady collected me for another bungee jump. We took a Skyline Gondola 1200 ft (400 metres) up to the jump site, and I felt the cool, still evening air. I was introduced to the jumping instructor. Once again, I was weighed, and then climbed onto the platform. The ledge protruded over the town. This bungee jump was 150 ft (47 metres). I was given a body harness with a winch attached, no ankle strap. The instructor said he would line me up, and when I was ready, I was to run off the edge. When he started recording the video, I smiled and jumped off without any hesitation. I fell freely for some seconds and then bounced. The impact on my body was less powerful than on my previous jump, although it was still a smack and my back took the brunt of the force. I bounced twice and then began swinging through the air. A climbing clip, connected to a rope, was sent down, which I had to attach to my harness. This took some doing! Once I had the clip attached, I was winched back up to the ledge.

The instructor said, "How was that, Tony?"

"Great. Bloody wicked," I replied.

He uncoupled the bungee rope and took me to the Ledge Sky Swing, situated on a higher platform. This time, I just had to step off sideways, and I would swing across a round wire ring in the sky. The Swing had an automatic winch attached that would pull me back to the platform after I stopped swinging.

I stood on a box to give me a better drop when I stepped off. The cable was attached to my harness and, after a few seconds, I stepped sideways, dropped like a stone, and slewed to the side. The harness caught me and I began to swing. After the rush of the bungee jump, this was gentle. I swung slowly across the sky sensing the silence of the night.

After about five minutes, I was winched back to the platform. The instructor returned me to ground level and gave me directions to the pub I had visited the evening before. It was around 10 pm, and when I reached the pub most of the gang had left, so I went to the World Bar, where I found the whole group.

I went straight to the bar and a girl gave me a shot of vodka. She said, "You have to stand on a table and strip."

Paul one said, "Are you up for that Tony?"

I grinned and said, "Fuckin' yeah."

The place was jumping and the music was booming. The girls said, "We want to see your manhood."

I said, "No problem, baby." I climbed on the table, held up the shot glass, smiled and dropped my shorts and boxers. I stood there with my genitals dangling for everyone to see and knocked back the vodka. I said, "Go on have a good look." My backside was on view for the bar girls... I pulled my clothes back up and jumped backwards off the table, feeling like a true champion.

When the World Bar closed, Cain took us to a few

other bars. The drinking lasted until 6.30 am.

Around 8 am that same morning, I was dragged out of bed by one of the hostel staff, to do yet another bungee jump. An A.J. Hackett team member drove me to the site. The Nevis bungee is in a gorge and is reached by cable car; the bungee pod itself was in the middle of the large Nevis River. I was knackered; I had only slept an hour and a half and was still drunk, although I didn't really feel it.

I was weighed, and someone said, "Tony you have lost 2 kg!"

I said, "How can that be, it should have increased with all my drinking!"

I put on a body harness and a group of us, including instructors, took the cable car to the pod.

This was the biggest bungee jump in New Zealand at the time, 405 ft (135 metres). A gigantic jump! The cable car shook crossing the gorge and that was just the start! The metal gantry moved constantly with the wind and the vibration from the river, which added to the excitement. We were in the middle of nowhere, with huge jagged rock walls on each side and a panoramic view of the entire area – it was magnificent. I had to sit on a huge padded seat while I had my ankles strapped together. I had support on my ankles and the harness was an extra precaution. He showed me where to hold on before giving me a second rope; after the first bounce, I was to pull this chord and my ankles would separate. If I did this just before the second bounce, it would be a fantastic experience.

I was then taken slowly to the edge and I said, "This

is the big one..." to the camera.

The guy yelled, "Ready?" Then he said "One, two, three, bungee!"

I didn't move. My brain was still scrambled, so the guy tapped me and I jumped. This time I had a good ten seconds freefall before the real fun began. I took the first bounce, which was massive, and my body felt like it had been hit by a freight train. Slam, and bounce! Every muscle felt like it was being pummelled. Then I was falling again, twisting. I managed to find and pull the chord just seconds before the next recoil. I bounced, and my ankles separated. What a rush and an explosion – my body didn't know what was happening. Each drop was huge and each bounce was enormous. I screamed and swore with joy. It cleared my head. After the third bounce, the bungee cord slackened and I sat in my harness waiting for the winch cable to be lowered so I could attach myself and be pulled back to the top.

When I returned to the platform, I was greeted once more like a hero. "How was it, Tony?" one guy asked.

I said, "Wahoo, man, it was bloody great!" I removed the gear and waited for the others to jump before we took the cable car back to land.

The following morning I arrived in reception to wait for the bus to Milford Sound, but it never arrived. I waited until 8 am and then asked the female receptionist to ring the office and find out what had happened. I was informed that they had forgotten to collect me. I asked if the bus could return, but it was gone. I later went to the travel office to rearrange the excursion, and organised a climbing and rope swing activity, and the bungee rocket for that day.

A friendly, muscular guy, who ran the climbing activity, met me around 11 am. There were five or six different apparatus in an area of secluded woodland. Whilst I was putting a harness on and fitting my helmet, the guy described the activities to me. Most consisted of climbing a vertical wooden post that had horseshoe shaped metal hoops along them. Each post was about 8 ft, just less than 3 metres high. My first activity consisted of climbing this post and then standing on top. I ascended easily enough, and once at the top, I put my stomach on the post head and levered myself into a kneeling position. Then I stretched my arms out to provide balance and stood up. The next task was a climbing wall, or a rope bridge; I attempted the rope bridge first. Again, I climbed the post, but this time upon reaching the top, I had to swing round and put my feet onto a single horizontal rope, hold onto two adjacent ropes and walk to the other end.

I accomplished that easily enough, but the climbing wall was another matter. I negotiated the post and then walked sideways along one rope hanging onto two higher ropes. When I reached the climbing wall, my strength went. I had to stretch a long distance and the bricks were too small to grip.

Next, there was another rope bridge, but this only had one support rope and was at a different angle to the one I walked along earlier. The rope I was walking gradually sloped towards the ground, and when I neared the end, there was a series of rope swings that I had to grab, and move from each rope whilst keeping my balance. I almost achieved it, but fell off while trying to reach one of the suspended ropes. There were two final events, a high wooden plank to walk, one with a rope to hold and another without. I did the first one and then finished; I was knackered and my legs and lungs were hurting – not to mention my fingers that were sore from the ropes. It was an enjoyable challenge.

I had my Rocket bungee on the outskirts of town. Two friendly guys told me how it operated and I was strapped into a large object that resembled a space ball. I was told not to touch anything. This was all caught on a video camera that was in the Rocket with me. Two bungee chords are connected to the rocket and stretched taught over a pair of high towers, and are held secure by large metal hooks. I removed my hearing aids, and then waited. The towers were 150 ft (50 metres) high. I didn't know what would happen. The men pushed the ball over on its side and I was upside down. They released the hooks and suddenly, without warning, I took off.

The force was terrific; I came out of my seat although the straps held me down. I said, "Fuck! Oh, shit." The look on my face must have been one of complete shock and surprise. I went about 210 ft (70 metres) into the air, before gently subsiding to the ground. The rush of the ball taking off was tremendous and a real surprise. It was good, if not better, than some of the bungee jumps. The guys asked me how it was. I replied, "Bloody brilliant."

Milford Sound
The following day I managed to catch the tour coach to Milford Sound. We had a grumpy, serious Maori driver for the three-hour journey along the scenic coast to the

Fiordland National Park.

The Sound is a fjord, surrounded by sheer rock faces, which rise 3,900 ft (1,200 metres) or more on each side. The sound flows 9 miles (15 km) inland from the Tasman Sea. I went there to experience the wildlife and the spectacular waterfalls. On the coach I met a young American girl who was a marine biology student. At Milford, we boarded a catamaran of the Red Boat Cruise Company for a two-hour sightseeing trip around the Fjord. My companion and I sat on deck and she described the idyllic scenery of the water's colours of blue and green against the darker background of the magnificent cliffs and mountains. The landscape and Sound were formed by the submergence of Mitres Peak mountain range, through the process of subduction over thousands of years.

A commentary informed everyone about the natural history as we first cruised down the south side of the fjord, passing such sights as Lady Bowen Falls, the highest permanent waterfall in the Sound, Cemetery Point, which has three burials and Sinbad Gully, a hanging valley in between impressive cliffs. When the catamaran reached Dale Point, the entrance-exit of the fjord, we ventured briefly into the Tasman Sea. The return journey took us up the north side of the Sound where we were soaked by the powerful spray of Stirling Falls, which was huge after recent heavy rain.

We stopped at Milford Deep Underwater Observatory in Harrison Cove. My American friend and I went about 30 ft (10 metres) under the sea to explore. We entered a dark room that had windows to view the sea life. She explained there were black and red coral, which was unusual, as they are normally found at lower depths. She also spotted sea stars, horse mussels and many different species of fish. We spent about twenty minutes in the observatory before returning to the catamaran.

On the journey back to the harbour, I was splashed by more waterfalls, which according to my friend, sparkled in the sun. She painted a vivid picture for me, as we cruised up the final part of the fjord: the majestic mountain peaks of Mitres, Lion and Elephant, the higher mountains of snow-capped Pembroke and the Sheerdown Range keeping watch in the distance. After docking, we returned to the coach for the long, slow journey back to Queenstown.

It was Cain's last evening in town and he was having a few drinks before leaving on his next journey. He had been a wonderful companion; he arranged events, constantly bought me drinks and was a good laugh. The next morning I had my 'awesome foursome', beginning with a return to the Nevis Highwire bungee. I went to the gorge with about twenty others, was weighed, as always, before doing the bungee again.

The instructor remembered me, and said, "Just like before, Tony."

I jumped – this time with no hesitation. The thrill was still fantastic, although on the second bounce, I failed to part my ankles and had to wait for the last bounce.

Next came the famous Shotover Jet experience!

About a dozen of us piled into this huge jet boat named "Big Red". We were each given a life jacket and a helmet. I got a seat near the front on the left and we took off up the Shotover River. We sped along, skimming past rocks and twisting through the narrow canyons. The driver made several 360° spins and we were all drenched! We returned to shore and were driven to a heli-pad where some of us, including myself, flew to the Kawarau River for the white water rafting. I boarded a coach with my own guide. Most of the group were driven to the riverside, whilst six others and I flew in the chopper. However, first we had to negotiate a narrow rock shelf that was just wide enough for the bus. If the driver had made any mistake, we would be at the bottom of the gorge! I heard many of the passengers gasp at the sight before us. Safely across, my group waited for the helicopter to arrive. I heard it land – that racket is unmistakable! We were given helmets, climbed aboard and fifteen minutes later, after a disappointing ride, we landed by the river.

The rafting trip was excellent and worth paying extra for a personal guide. We were given the usual equipment for a four hour, afternoon rafting excursion. There were six of us, including the two guides. We set off once we had been given a safety drill and were shown some rafting techniques. I sat on the left side near the back. We splashed down river into some spectacular rapids. The river was low and showed the rocks. The rapids were level 2 or 3. We passed through ten rapids, getting drenched several times. We finished by going through a rock tunnel and descending into a massive wave, where we were told to get down, and hold on. We exited the tunnel and paddled straight into a rapid where the water exploded everywhere – completely drenching us; it was a fantastic conclusion to the day. The next morning Andy, another of the Kiwi Experience bus drivers I had become friendly with, collected me and we drove to Dunedin, where I began another journey... to the bottom of New Zealand

Dunedin and Invercargill
We travelled to Dunedin, stopping in the small town of Cromwell for lunch, and arrived in the mountainous city around 4 pm. By then the wind had increased and the clouds had darkened. Before driving to the city centre we stopped on Baldwin Street, which is reputed to be the steepest street in the world – it felt almost vertical. A Japanese girl and I were deposited at the HI, a very cheap place, only $4 per night. This hostel was almost empty, somewhat shabby and also closed during the day.

A guy in his late fifties collected the Japanese girl and myself and we were driven to the exposed Otago Peninsula for a pre-arranged tour. The area was wild with a rough, undulating terrain, where the land protruded into the Pacific Ocean. A strong, cold, wind blew and the energy of the peninsula was astounding.

At the rock cliff edge, known as Lover's Leap, we looked down on a picture of wildlife; there were Yellow-eye Penguins and shags that cried and dived for fish. There were small black seals that swam long distances to catch their food. At Taiaroa Head, our guide told us about the Northern Royal Albatross breeding colony and I heard several of the birds fly overhead. I heard the sea crashing against the bottom of the rocks and took in the atmosphere of the expanse around me, which I found beautiful. My blindness meant I was more alert and used my other senses to absorb the natural environment. I had the open expanse and the wild elements to paint my mental picture. This is what I mean about it being beautiful. I could visualise the expanse of the area through the animal's calls, plus the sea and wind. But it was the energy of the area which really struck me; strong but somehow remote. The space was conveyed to me through my skin and face. It was magnificent, cold, bleak and dangerous – most definitely beautiful.

The torrential rain prevented me from exploring Dunedin, so I continued along the coast.

Invercargill
To reach the bottom of South Island, we drove along the south east coast, which was spectacular. We went through The Catlins and stopped several times to admire the scenery. We took a walk through a fossilized forest near the sea, where fur seals and dolphins were spotted off shore.

We arrived in Invercargill, New Zealand's most southern and western city, around early evening. Most people continued around the coast and onwards, but another guy and I decided to spend the night in a small hostel that was located above a nightclub. The bus driver organised my itinerary, including my one night stay in Invercargill, my return ferry ticket to Stewart Island, and my accommodation on the island. I was told that I would need to take food and cash, as Stewart had a simplistic culture.

Invercargill was uninteresting; there was a HI, but it was a 4 mile (6 km) walk from the rough city. The other guy who stayed at the independent hostel helped me buy provisions for the trip ahead. I rose early the next morning, took a bus to the small port of Bluff, and caught a ferry to Stewart Island.

Stewart Island

I arrived around 10 am after an hour's sailing and took a taxi to the hostel. The accommodation was quiet, near the ferry port, along a small gravel path, and just a five-minute walk from a hotel and bar. It was only a two-minute stroll from the beach. I paid cash for three night's stay and settled in. The hostel comprised of a main house with additional accommodation blocks, and a small yard separated the buildings. I stashed my food in the kitchen and went exploring.

At the tourist information centre I was informed bird watching tours were available that day. In the afternoon, the tour guide, a lovely lady in her late fifties, collected me in a small open top peddle car. I climbed in through an open window just like they did in *The Dukes of Hazard,* a TV series that I used to love. The lady was really friendly and extremely knowledgeable about the area and its nature. She seemed impressed that I was travelling independently around the world.

We drove to a small harbour and were met by a Swedish couple and their young son. The lady told us she was of European and Maori descent, so we were greeted by touching noses. We boarded a motorboat for a short ride to Ulva Island Bird Sanctuary.

Following a trail through the rain forest the guide told us about the island's bird life. Many birds in New Zealand are non-flying – they had no natural predator until humans arrived. Ulva had been cleared of predators and many bird species had returned to what was their natural habitat.

The walk along the dry, wooded trail through the forest was interesting; we traversed several naturally made steps. I touched some of the large, Silver Fern leaves that our guide said the Maori used as toilet paper whenever they were in the bush. I heard birds talking and calling all around us. Our guide was able to recognise each species by their call – it was amazing. It was a peaceful, relaxing, and informative afternoon. Our walk took us down to a beach where we rested. Incredibly, a bird came and sat on the sand, just inches from my hand. We took a different route back to the boat, where we saw some prehistoric trees.

The next day I ventured down to the shore and began tracing the coast. I followed the sounds of the sea and wondered where it would take me. Stewart Island is like travelling back in time forty years. People talk to each other, say hello, are pleasant to one another, smile and appear friendly. Life is slower. The activities on the island are about survival, not capitalism.

I hardly heard a vehicle on my walk; it was completely quiet, except for the sea crashing on the rocks close by. I stopped frequently to explore the rock edge with my cane, feeling for the difference in texture and size.

I became completely submerged in these beautiful surroundings. When the hill I was climbing became too steep for me I retraced my steps.

The following afternoon I went fishing. I was collected around 1 pm and taken to the harbour where I boarded a fishing boat and was given a raincoat to keep me dry. The captain, a friendly man, gave me a long rope with a hook on the end, which he let me feel. He said he would tie a knot some distance from the end, as he was worried about me getting the hook in my hands. There were eight of us on board, and when we reached a particular point, I dropped my line. I felt a tug and pulled the rope in quickly, but had caught nothing. After several attempts, we moved to a better spot and repeated the practice.

This time I was more successful – we all were. My second attempt caught my first fish, which was large and slimy. Then they came up in abundance; I even got two on the same line at one point. We used live worms for bait and I managed to catch eight fish, which we shared.

I was able to take six fish back to the hostel. The boat's crew gutted and skinned them for me. I had a grand time, standing by the rail, pulling my rope line through my fingers with the sea spray hitting my face. I cut both my thumbs, but this goes with the job. We were at sea for around four hours. We finished fishing and had a fast and bumpy but enjoyable ride back to shore.

I visited the nearby fish shop and asked the owner if he would cook my fish for me. I offered to pay and prompted him by saying, "They don't want me to burn down the hostel!" He agreed and I paid him $1 per fish. That night I had a delicious meal of cod and bread. The boat back to South Island was leaving the following afternoon, so I spent the day by the beach.

Back in Invercargill, I went to the pub opposite the hostel to wait for the Kiwi Experience bus. The driver once again was Andy, and on seeing me, gave me a huge hug. We all climbed aboard and went to the coastal town of Riverton for one night.

Te Anau, Queenstown and Christchurch

After breakfast, we visited the Hook's sea lions. A small group of us, including Andy, walked across a long beach to where they lay in the sun. We were able to get really close to them, and I asked if we could touch one.

Andy said, "They might eat you, Tony!"

We stood about 9 ft (3 metres) from them. They could kill a human if they attacked, and move with lightening speed, especially in the water. There was one male lying right in front of us. He was about 6 ft (2 metres) long and weighed around 420 lbs (200 kg). You could smell them before you saw them as they stank!

Eventually, we reached the lake town of Te Anau, arriving late afternoon in sunny weather. During the last two weeks I experienced the best weather of my entire trip around New Zealand. I stayed at a small HI, run by an inquisitive lady who was in her late fifties. Here I chilled for two days. The small lake town was quiet and relaxing. I had a horse ride on my first evening. I was collected around 6 pm and taken to some stables in the countryside, owned by a lovely young lady who took me riding for three hours. I said I had ridden before, so saddled up. She led and I followed. We talked quietly as we rode, with the warm evening sun on our backs. We crossed several fields and descended a rocky path that became very steep in places. It was a challenging ride, but enjoyable.

I booked a canoe trip for the next day, but unfortunately missed the pick up. I walked around part of lake Te Anau, New Zealand's second largest lake in surface area at 132.81 square miles (3442 km). It is the largest lake in South Island. In the afternoon, I caught the Kiwi Experience bus to Queenstown.

Queenstown: Part Two

I returned to the HI and later met up with Andy and Sally. Andy suggested I went river boarding with him to which I agreed. I asked about going rally driving and Sally said she knew a guy who owned a rally car and would try to organise that for me.

The next day I went to the Kiwi Experience office to see old friends and book some more activities. I organised the Pipeline Bungee jump in Skipper's Canyon for that day. I also booked an aerobatic plane trip. I wanted to pump more adrenalin! I was taken to Skippers Canyon at the head of the Shotover River. The bus had to cross that dangerously narrow ledge again. At the site, I was again weighed and greeted by the instructors, who had heard of my reputation. I said, "I want to do this one backwards," and they agreed. It was a 335 ft (102 metre) bungee with only an ankle support. I was strapped up as usual, and they started filming. Once on the edge, I was turned around so that I faced backwards towards the long narrow canyon of jagged rock; I was then tapped three times and dived off. I dropped with a generous freefall, then smack, the rope recoiled and I bounced aggressively. It was sensational! I was kicked in the small of my back by the force, and bounced again. The scenery was a picture of natural rock dissected by the river. The jump was terrific in such spectacular scenery. I knew the area was stunning because of the echo and energy that emanated from the rock canyon. After three or four bounces, while twisting and turning upside down, I was slowly lowered into a motor boat, then driven to the shore and taken out of the canyon by jeep. The bungee was tremendous and probably the best of the jumps I performed in New Zealand.

I returned to town and waited to see if there would be any good flying weather. I was in luck; there was no rain and only a slight wind. Another guy and I were taken to the airport, where our pilot told us about the plane and what would happen. I was kitted out in a jumpsuit and given a helmet and goggles. I went up twenty minutes after the other guy had flown.

The plane was a small two-man machine. I sat in front of the pilot and could hear him, but he couldn't hear me. I had to climb into a small compartment with a bucket seat, where he strapped me in. He told me to stick up my thumb if I was ok, and reverse it if I was not. Then he got in and we took off.

We climbed to about 5,000 ft (1,650 metres) where we levelled out and the pilot began a slow barrel roll, which put me upside down. I signalled my enjoyment. It was a strange feeling, as even though we were flying at a great speed it still felt slow. We began to do some loops and I felt the sensation of rolling forwards. He attempted a backward loop, but aborted it when he could feel himself beginning to black out. It was great – damned hot, but exhilarating and unfortunately over too quickly.

We did one almost vertical dive, pulling back up at

the last moment. The sensations were thrilling. Then as suddenly as it had begun, it was over and we were back on terra firma.

The next morning a lady took me to Cardona Adventure Park in the mountains. She told me about the rally car and the track they had. She informed the instructor I liked to go fast and wasn't afraid of danger. I paid $160, which I thought was reasonable, especially with collection from Queenstown and back.

I was kitted out in fire-safety gear, a body suit, helmet and gloves. It was a hot day and all this gear made me sweat profusely. I climbed into the front passenger seat of the rally car, which was built like a Land Rover. My guide and I drove around a racetrack at top speed for about ten minutes. The car jumped a couple of bumps on the track and I felt each one, which was tremendous. We reached 70 miles per hour (112 kilometres per hour) at one point. We took a long bend and I felt the car almost tip over – this was even more exhilarating. As usual, this experience was over too quickly for me. I was becoming an adrenalin junkie!

In the afternoon, I went river boarding. The lady dropped me at Andy's office in town and about twelve of us were driven to the Kawarau River in a mini-bus, while Andy explained the event. Once we arrived, I put on a large wetsuit and walked down to the river. This was quite difficult as there were many rocks and boulders, plus it was very hot. River boarding is swimming under rapids on a small board, wearing rubber flippers to propel you. Andy advised us to stay in the middle of the river, so that the current would carry us along. I entered the cool water and Andy pushed me under to see if I liked it. I found it bearable, but wasn't ecstatic about it.

I lay on my board and began to kick my feet, but I hadn't gone five yards when I stopped and said, "Sorry, Andy, my back has gone. I'm completely out of strength."

I was honest about it, and realised that it was better to stop now rather than when approaching a large and dangerous rapid. I'd had a go and decided that it was not for me, but at least I had tried it. I guessed I'd found my limit.

I was helped out of the water and with one of the guides, climbed back up the rocks to the van. I stripped off my gear and we drove down to collect the guys after their first run, then returned them to the top for their second swim. When everyone finished, I was deposited at the hostel where I prepared to leave for my final destination in New Zealand.

That night I had a couple of beers with Andy and Sally and then went to the World Bar for one last blast, before heading to Christchurch. I bought a beer and went to find a seat. I put my drink on a table and this girl said, "Hi" and touched my arm. We began talking and she said she had seen me around before. I asked where she was from and what she looked like. She said she was from Swindon in the West Country. I grinned and told her that I came from Weston-super-Mare. I liked her immediately and she let me feel her hair and face. She had piercings everywhere, six in each ear, one in her nose and a long tongue stud. Then she let me touch the hoops in her nipples, which I enjoyed. I put my hands on her legs as we talked and then I kissed her. She was lovely, slightly taller than me, with smooth skin and a friendly personality. We drank and talked; I moved my hands around her body seductively.

She said, "Tony, not in here, let's go outside."

I was very excited and really aroused. I had pulled a genuine girl. We went to some secluded steps and had some fun! We eventually rejoined the party until around 3 am, when we left the World Bar and walked around the town holding hands.

Her friends returned to their hostel and one of them said, "Tony, bring her home before 7 am."

I said, "Yes," and smiled.

We went by the lake, sat on a bench, kissed and talked while I stroked her soft hair. She was warm, with her strong, sexy legs beside mine. The night was hot, and it felt romantic. We eventually made love on the grass. We kissed for a bit then got dressed and searched for a taxi. We sat in the back holding hands and kissing; I could not get enough of her! Finally, she was dropped at her hostel. We exchanged emails and one last kiss before I went to the HI.

I got a few hours sleep and woke early that same morning to catch the Kiwi Experience bus to Christchurch on the east coast.

Around 7 pm, as the sun was setting, I entered the hostel, said I had a reservation, and was shown to an upstairs dorm. It was a relaxing place with a comfortable lounge. I spent two brief days in South Island's largest city, exploring the music shops.

I finally caught my early morning flight back to Australia for some more fun.

Chapter 11

Australia: the West Coast

I had ten more days in Australia; it was now February 2002. I spent two days in Sydney and then went to Perth, on the west coast. I chose to fly instead of going by bus, since they were both the same price, but the bus took three and a half days one way. The flight took eight hours with a three-hour time reversal.

Perth

I arrived in Perth quite late in the evening, caught a bus to the hostel and was welcomed by a friendly young receptionist. It was a cramped place with tiny dorms. There were ten bunks squeezed into a room that had little space for manoeuvre! There was only a top bunk left for me. Once I settled in and made my bed, I enquired about tours. I knew about the Swan River and had heard that Fremantle was only one hour away. There were several trips available into the desert. However, I was low on money so I opted for a city tour that included going to the Indian Ocean. I wanted to swim in it! I also wanted to visit the Western Australian Cricket Academy (WACA), one of the fastest cricket pitches in the world. I had listened to the West Indian fast bowlers destroy Alan Border's team on this pitch in less than two days, back in 1990. It was lethal if you had pace, and this was something Dennis Lilley discovered during his time there.

My city tour began with a visit to a sanctuary for abandoned animals – kangaroos and wallabies mainly. An English guy and I were driven around in tremendous heat in a van that, luckily, had air conditioning. At the park, two ladies gave a talk about the animals and I was able to hold a baby possum and a small wallaby. One of the ladies described how they made small bags, like pouches, to keep the babies warm. The other lady explained how the wallaby sucked on his own balls for comfort! We moved on to an Aborigine centre similar to the one I visited in Alice Springs, but this time we were treated to a musical demonstration. The Aborigine band gave a short talk about the musical pieces they were to play and about the instruments they used, made from eucalyptus trees. I was able to touch the instruments. There were painted didgeridoos and boomerangs for sale, which were impressive and skilfully made.

In the afternoon we went to the Indian Ocean where I sat on some steps in the blazing heat and listened to the sea's powerful surge. I stripped off and stepped in briefly, allowing the warm water to reach my knees, the strong current rushing over my skin and the waves pushing me backwards powerfully. At least I had been in the Indian Ocean! We had ice cream before the tour finished.

Back at the hostel, I enquired how to get to the WACA and the owner arranged to take me there. The receptionist took me to a nearby travel agency. I wished to go to Fremantle and then travel onto Bunbury, where it was possible to see dolphins. I decided to travel by train, as it was cheaper than the bus.

Swan beer is drunk in Perth: it is quite strong and the most expensive in Australia. Perth is expensive because there are no other major cities in near proximity to create competitive trading.

I chatted with some guys in the hostel's backyard. Most of them were from England and there was one Scottish guy. We all decided to visit a bar called Aberdeen, several blocks from the hostel. Someone ordered a few jugs; I enjoyed the Swan beer and the bar's atmosphere. I was really drunk when I returned to the hostel around 1 am. One of the other guys joined me and we had several more beers before I eventually turned in.

It was during the early hours that I decided I needed the toilet. The bunk bed had no ladder, so I put my feet on the bottom bunk and tried to slide down, but I fell and smacked my left cheek on a wooden sideboard. I didn't feel a thing; I got up from the floor, went to the toilet with blood dripping everywhere, and then returned to bed.

The next morning the owner came to wake me to take me to the WACA for our tour. He took one look at me and said, "Tony what the fuck happened to you? You've got blood everywhere."

I smiled, felt my cheek and replied, "I was in a fight with Mike Tyson and I won!"

There was blood all over my face, on the sheets and the large cut to my left cheek would not stop bleeding. The owner took me to the local hospital where I was eventually seen by a doctor, who put six stitches in my cheek, which became a nice scar! I never did get to the WACA.

I chatted with an English girl who travelled globally with her job. The following day she and her boyfriend accompanied me on a boat ride on the Swan River. We arrived at the river with moments to spare for the cruise. It was a slow, relaxing ride and took an hour each way.

After the cruise, we wandered back into town and went to a park that had a large lake in the middle. We walked around the park and visited the Perth War Memorial, which interested me. We went to the lake and put our feet in – it was cool and inviting. That evening I found a bar that had live jazz and a band with a female vocalist. She was good. I sat at the bar, drank expensive Swan beer at $6 a bottle and enjoyed myself.

Fremantle

I took a train to Fremantle, where I stayed for two uninteresting nights. I spent my only day walking along the coast road, listening to the ocean crashing below with the blazing sun on my naked back. I passed an evening in a quiet pub which, to my astonishment, closed early!

Bunbury

Bunbury was delightful. The three hour train journey from Perth was relaxing. An elderly couple owned the tiny hostel where I spent the night. I briefly explored the small town, finding a couple of bars, shops and restaurants in a nearby main street. Early the next morning the owner took me to the beach to see if the dolphins were about.

I sat on the beach for a couple of hours and waited, but the dolphins had either arrived early or decided not to show that morning. If the dolphins had been there, I would have been able to stand in the water and have them swim between my legs. A local who had also waited for the dolphins gave me a lift to the railway station.

I spent a final night in Perth before returning to Sydney, where I caught my flight to South East Asia and the last leg of that magnificent journey.

Chapter 12

South East Asia – the Nations of Dreams

South East Asia (SEA) is one of the world's magical regions. It contains a dynasty of qualities and since 1995, certainly since 2000, it has been a haven to many travellers and tourists, and is more diverse than many people believe. Extensively, the region contains Brunei, Burma (Union of Myanmar), Cambodia, Indonesia, Laos, Malaysia, Papua New Guinea, Philippines, Singapore, Thailand, Timor East, and Vietnam. It doesn't include The People's Republic of China (PRC), although the southern part lies within the same latitude.

Of all the countries mentioned, I only visited Vietnam and Thailand. In hindsight, I should have travelled further, but I wasn't as confident then as I am now and by the time I arrived in SEA I was tired, low on funds and ready to go home. The main reason for this entire trip was to reach and explore the Democratic Republic of Vietnam (DRV). My reasons were part historical and academic and part curiosity.

I first went to Thailand. To get to Vietnam or any of the other countries in that region, you usually had to go via Bangkok, Thailand's capital. I arrived in Bangkok late in the evening after a ten-hour flight from Australia.

I had previously arranged a one-night stay in a hotel near the airport, intending to fly to Vietnam the next day. At Bangkok International Airport I was met and taken, along with another guest, to the hotel. I had a voucher for my stay, but on arrival at the hotel I was unable to locate it. Unfortunately, most of the staff couldn't speak English. My documents were searched and, thankfully, a copy of the voucher was found. I was shown up to a luxurious room that had a large double bed, a TV and a fridge that contained a variety of beverages.

The man said, "If you need anything, just call," with emphasis on the word anything!

The next morning I was escorted back to the airport to catch my two-hour flight to Ho Chi Minh City in the south of Vietnam. I had heard that passing through customs could be problematic and that bribes were commonplace, so visitors should be cautious. My trip was in 2002 and at that time there were still very few tourists travelling to Vietnam. Now it has become more accessible, which has a double effect – on the positive side it creates badly needed income for the country, but on the negative side the added influx of people damages its peacefulness and beauty.

I had purchased my 30-day visa previously in the UK, so passing through customs was non-eventful. I had booked accommodation in Vietnam and the owner of the guesthouse expected me. There were no established hostels in Vietnam when I visited. The owner emailed my Mum to obtain my flight number and time of arrival, and sent someone to meet me. However, we must have missed each other at the arrival gate. I was taken as far as customs by the airport staff and then left to my own devices. I met a young Vietnamese lady who was returning from working in Australia to visit her family for the Tet holiday. She helped me through customs and luggage collection and, when I told her my destination, she rang the guesthouse and received further directions. The lady helped me change my US dollars to Vietnamese Dong, which was approximately 22,000 to £1 and 30,000 to $1 in early 2002.

We shared a taxi that dropped me at my guesthouse, and the lady gave me an address card and told me to ring her if I had any trouble. The airport was far from the city, and I felt the heat just as I had felt the humidity in Bangkok. It was slightly less intense in Vietnam as it was their winter, but the car fumes were heavy.

At my allotted arrival point I went into an apartment with my pack, where an old man took me up some stairs and in broken English, asked me to wait. After several minutes, a younger man introduced himself telling me to call him Tee, and took me across the road and into his guesthouse.

Ho Chi Minh City (Saigon)

I felt exhausted but elated – I had arrived in Saigon, the city's former name. Tee showed me to a simple self-contained bedroom-bathroom that was up several flights of concrete steps. He brought in a TV; he was very polite and friendly and his English was excellent. I spoke to him carefully and slowly. Tee was small and thin. His mum owned the guesthouse and he and his girlfriend ran it for her. I stayed for a week, and he told me to pay later, saying, "No problem, Mr Tony."

The house was large and cool downstairs and was open, just as I had imagined it, and everything was made of wood. When I came downstairs, Tee showed me to a large chair. He served coffee the Vietnamese way – producing a small glass cup that had a flame under it which he placed in front of me on the table. His girlfriend, who undertook the house chores and the cooking, poured the hot water into the cup.

I asked Tee what excursions were available and he suggested that one of his friends take me around the city on a motorbike for $1 an hour. There were possible excursions to the Mekong Delta and to the Cuchi Tunnels. The tunnels were what the North Vietnamese Army (NVA) and Viet Cong gorillas (VC) had used during the war against the US and South Vietnamese in the 1960s and early 1970s. Tee kindly organised both tours for me. I had an evening meal of spring rolls with rice mixed with meat, followed by a bowl of noodle soup. It was the best food I have ever eaten. I decided I'd return there the next day for the food alone, although the people were also delightful.

Tee took me to a local bar on his small moped. I sat on the back and held on tight, and once I got my balance, I felt perfectly safe. The locals ride around with their entire families on these mopeds. The streets were small and narrow with cracked pavements and plenty of rubbish. However, the neighbourhood where I stayed was mainly quiet. It was constantly humid, there was no wind and I could smell the stench of the city emanating from the river. Tee told me to wear my bum bag around

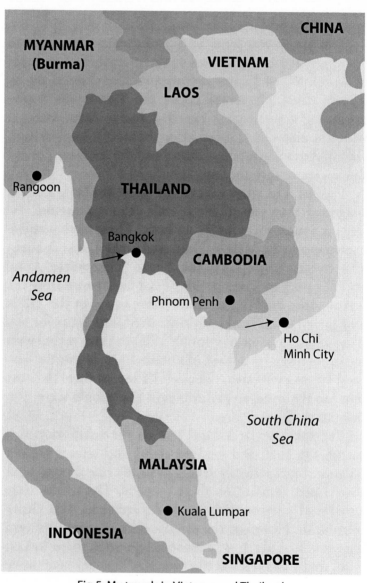

Fig 5: My travels in Vietnam and Thailand

my stomach covered by my t-shirt for safety. After a two-minute bike ride, I was deposited outside the bar. Tee showed me to the door and asked a guy to look after me. He gave me the address and told me that I could find a bike taxi outside and return any time.

I pushed through the dense crowd to the bar and ordered a bottle of Saigon beer. It's not strong but tastes good and cost $1 a bottle. I had a couple and then got the taxi bike back to the hostel. This routine occurred each night and on my second evening I met an American music student who was in Vietnam on a college exchange. I met him coming out of the small, dingy toilet, and he showed me back to my seat at the bar. We struck up a conversation. I called him the 'Quiet American' as in Graham Green's novel *The Quiet American* (1955); he really was quiet by American standards! We discussed music, and he was amazed that I was travelling alone.

Ho Chi Minh City is the largest city in the south and was once the capital. Hanoi in the north is now Vietnam's capital. Ho Chi Minh was a socialist revolutionary who organized the Vietnamese people, established the Communist party and directed the fight for independence. He died in 1969 before his vision was fulfilled. When the communists captured Saigon on 30th April 1975, the city was renamed in recognition of his vision and ideology – although the locals still call the city Saigon.

When I was there, it was Tet holiday, a religious festival when families congregate, eat and pray together. Vietnam is largely a Buddhist country and they are a very proud and respectful people. Therefore, Tee was not sure what places would be open for me to visit. The Tet festival on 31st January 1968 was used by the North Vietnamese Army to surmount a countrywide surprise attack on the south, getting as far as inside the US Embassy in Saigon. This became a political victory for the DRV and caused major political disturbances in the US government. However, it was not a military victory for the north, and the Viet Cong were almost depleted. I had already studied this, hence my reason for visiting during Tet.

I woke early due to the heat. Breakfast consisted of strong coffee and French bread with jam. Tee asked what I wished to do and about my knowledge of Vietnam. I asked him about his culture and also about the war. His parents remembered it well. His mother was lovely, quiet, but strong. She said she had two sons, but was sad because she had no daughter and she had always longed for one.

After breakfast, Tee summoned a taxi bike. I visited a temple and the driver took me to where people prayed. He allowed me to touch a large pillar that was decorated with ornate carvings, before we descended the marbled steps and continued our tour. We also visited the war museum. Travelling by moped was an excellent way to get a feel for the city. The foul, sewage-like stench of the Saigon River emanated across the city. We had to meander through traffic; it was crazy. To cross a road in Vietnam, you don't expect the traffic to stop, because it never does. It flows slowly and you move with it, passing through gaps when they appear, and the traffic lights that do exist are simply ignored. It is precarious, but that's how traffic life operates in Vietnam. It's organised chaos, and thousands of mopeds weave in and out of the traffic with relish. I sweated constantly. My driver spoke some English, and he announced the old radio-TV centre and the police headquarters as we passed them. These had been well known during the war and were attacked regularly.

At the War Remnants Museum, I touched an American tank and its large gun barrel, and a huge, unexploded 15,00lbs (6,800 kg) bomb, kindly dropped by the American Air Force! There were several other captured American vehicles and aircraft on display in an outside courtyard. We went inside the museum, but there were mainly graphic pictures of war atrocities, the attack on the US Embassy in January 1968 and the fall of the city in 1975.

We took a tour around the palace, which had existed for at least two centuries. I was admitted free and paid for my guide. The palace, which had several different names and was re-built many times, had been used by a Vietnamese dynasty before the French arrived in the mid-nineteenth century. Several battles occurred with the indigenous people before they were overpowered and Vietnam, Cambodia and Laos were changed into what was called French Indochina. Vietnam was once three separate areas that consisted of Tonkin in the north, including the gulf, Anam in the central highlands and Cochin in the south, but the French created one province. They remained until the Japanese invaded in 1941. At the conclusion of World War II, Japanese military and French administrators were removed and the Vietnamese attempted to create their own country.

However, global politics intervened and the Indochina

wars began. First, against the French until they were suppressed; and then against the US who were also defeated. The Vietnamese even removed Chinese aggression and Cambodian infiltration. The DRV has been independent since May 1975 and still remains so. They have a communist/socialist government who, until the late 1980s, controlled the country ruthlessly. Many children didn't attend school, crop production was problematic and survival was difficult and still is today. Many people, most notably non-communists and those who had fought alongside the Americans, left in the late 1970s – they became known as the 'boat people'.

The French used the palace as their headquarters. The Japanese did likewise. The Americans used it to house the leader of South Vietnam from the late 1960s until the fall of Saigon.

The palace itself, which is now called Reunification Palace, was resplendent with huge high ceilings and white marble walls and pillars. It had at least three floors and many sections. I struggled to hear the guide because of the echo from the cavernous rooms.

Vietnam is on the lower level of developing world countries. People sleep on the streets; they beg in the bars and try to sell anything from books to wooden beads. Women carry babies in their arms, whilst little children hustle for money. However, the country has several exports – its chief commodities are rubber from the trees to make condoms and tyres, as well as rice and also metal such as tin.

When I was not on a tour, I spent my afternoons relaxing. The heat sapped my energy, as it was more humid than

Australia. Manoeuvring around the city independently was difficult. I could not speak the language and I didn't have the confidence to explore, as I did on later trips. My American friend met me one day and we explored the city. We began by having breakfast in a café, eggs followed by noodle soup, which was the best dish I have ever eaten – forget steak, or fish and chips, this was real cuisine – a large bowl of noodles with fish or beef, along with lots of hot vegetables. The juice came from cooking the meat. It was rich, hot, but not spicy, and very filling.

We then explored, walking through the market that smelt of rotting fruit, meat and vegetables. I touched some of the fruit; the oranges and melons were the size of basketballs! We avoided the meat, it was swarming with flies and the stench was horrendous, as it was left out in the heat of the day. There were flies everywhere, although I got used to them and swatted them with my hands. I was bitten at night by mosquitoes, but only sporadically. Vietnam, and the majority of southern Asia, has mosquitoes and in the tropical regions they carry malaria, but I used cream to repel them. The sand flies of Australia and New Zealand had been worse!

My friend and I walked through several of the squares. He described the different buildings, and we sat on a bench in a park during the afternoon. A man on a motorbike approached us and offered me sex. I replied, "Not with you, mate!"

Another person approached from behind us and began a conversation. When he realised my friend was American, he got excited and was delighted to meet him. You might think this funny after what the US military and government had inflicted upon Vietnam. However, I'm properly informed that they love Americans. Perhaps it is more of an economic fondness, but who can say.

Around mid-afternoon, I returned to the guesthouse after a relaxing, but long and hot day. I arranged to meet my friend in the bar that night. Once again Tee took me there and I had a meal that consisted of rice with meat, like a stew; it was rich and delicious, containing a variety of herbs and spices.

My tour to the tunnels took me into Vietnam's interior. I was collected early from the guesthouse and taken to the centre where I boarded a mini-bus. We drove along Highway 1, the main motorway out of Saigon. This was once the end of the Ho Chi Minh trail, a vast network of underground tunnels that stretched into Vietnam's interior and even went as far as Cambodia and Laos. We drove for about three hours, and stopped at a town for a religious royal demonstration, which was given by some local people who were dressed in coloured robes. They represented different parts of the Vietnamese royal court. We entered an old building with a balcony to see some of the performance where I met two Australian ladies. They said the coloured robes were beautiful, but I wasn't sure what was really happening.

One of the girls told me she saw a Vietnamese girl asleep on the ground, covered in dirt and flies and that she'd thought the girl was dead at first. This is what a developing country is like – the poverty is so evident. Our guide explained why the Americans and South Vietnamese failed to win the war, and provided a history in the process.

It took a good four hours altogether to reach Cuchi on the Cambodian border. A remake of the original tunnels was constructed with a series of military booby traps and other artefacts to explain elements of the wars to the tourists. Our guide demonstrated the operation of bombs. I was able to trigger one by snapping a string with my cane. A loud cap gun bang exploded and the guide said, "Tony's dead!"

Another trap was presented in the form of a wooden stick that clubbed a person on entering a closed room. I got to touch several torture devices. Our guide said the Americans had no chance because they could not identify different sections of the Vietnamese population, north or south, peasant or Viet Cong. During the day, a Vietnamese might be a cook for the US military and at night, he might sneak back and attack the camp. He also explained that the NVA was patient. A Vietnamese soldier could hide undercover for a week with nothing but water and a bag of rice, and would watch, as each day the same truck carrying perhaps sixteen American troops drove to the same spot on patrol. After several days of reconnaissance, the Vietnamese would destroy them with a single rocket grenade or mortar.

There were models of a farmer and his wife. They wore large hats and peasant clothes to illustrate the difficulty in identifying different sections of Vietnamese people. I descended a small ladder into a hole and, on hands and knees, I crawled through a replica of the tunnel. The original tunnels were half the height and size of these. Vietnamese people eat very little meat, unlike in western society, and subsequently are much smaller.

Several members of the group fired a machine gun. This experience was included in the tour. You could fire a bullet from an AK47 Russian made machine gun, which was the type preferred by the NVA and VC or an M16 used by the American forces. The AK47 is lighter and better in hot swampy conditions.

I asked to fire one, but our guide said, "You shoot tour guide!" and laughed. The guy in charge would not let me shoot, but he did allow me to hold both weapons. I asked what the target was and he said, "A picture of American!"

We also took a walk through the jungle, which was lined with traps and trip wires and found a small pit with a rope trap that took away a person's legs and left them hanging in the trees for the snakes and tigers to feast upon. I touched the gun barrel of a large tank, which the guide told us had been used during the capture of Saigon. Back in the city, I got a taxi bike to the guesthouse and had a long, cold shower to wash away the dirt. I met up with my American friend and told him about my day – he was impressed.

Around 1 am, he put me on a motorbike taxi and asked the driver to return me to my guesthouse. However, when we drove off the driver didn't turn for my street. Suddenly, another bike came alongside and we drove for several minutes. A guy asked me if I like 'bonk bonk' and a girl said, "Me give you good bonk bonk, very good. Love you all night!"

I wondered what I should do. If I refused they could kill me and still take my money. I therefore accepted, seeing no solution, and was curious to discover what would happen. We went to a small hotel. They told me if I didn't do it, they would return my money. I went in a room with the girl and had about forty minutes with her. They asked me if I had done it and when I nodded, they drove me back towards the city. Suddenly the bike stopped under an arch, I could tell because of the echo. They asked for money, I gave them what I thought they wanted, but they said "More, more…"

Finally, all I had was two dollars and they said that was okay. They kept reassuring me that it was fine; they would not rip me off.

"Okay, okay," one guy repeated, "You're our friend."

I was finally deposited at my accommodation and I banged on the door until it was opened. It was around 3 am, and I went to bed feeling slightly embarrassed more than anything, although somewhat different for the experience.

The next day, I went for my Mekong Delta tour, but when I arrived, the guide said there were too many people and I had to go the following day. Up to this point, Vietnam was the most difficult challenge I had faced travel wise, although, I believe, if I had wanted to travel through the country by bus I could have done so. However, getting around Saigon on foot was a different matter. Nevertheless, I definitely gained an experience.

I finally went to the Mekong Delta. This is an area mostly consisting of rice paddy fields and swamps interspersed by villages. Once again, we left Saigon via Highway 1, but this time ventured off into the bush. We visited a couple of villages, used a small boat at one point and went through a very wet paddy field. They are swamps filled with rainwater and are abundant with vegetation. They were good hiding places for the NVA and VC during the wars. The boat was a flat bottomed, square shaped vessel with a loud motor. The paddies are often shallow and this boat is ideal for navigating Vietnam's waterways.

We visited a rice cake factory and a jam processing plant, and were given gifts of fruit at several intervals. I put mine in my pack, conscious of the danger of eating foreign fruit, but I did try the rice cakes and the green tea. The tea tastes plain, but is easy to get used to. We spent the entire day in the Mekong, where the birds sang in the bush. I felt the remoteness of my surroundings and the closeness of the river to the small wooden houses and brick buildings; here was the developing world. The people talked. We had a meal in one place. There was rice, chicken and different bowls of vegetables and salad, which I avoided. Once we had finished exploring the Delta, we began our long, slow drive to the city.

I paid Tee for his hospitality and for the trips. The whole week cost around £100, meals, accommodation and excursions included. On my final morning, Tee arranged for a motorbike taxi to take me to the airport. This was about a forty-minute ride and cost me $3 – this was a lot better than the real taxi. However, once at the airport the fun began. I had to pay airport tax to leave the country and I didn't have enough dong, so I figured I could use a cash machine, but there were none in the airport. The nearest was back in the city, and I would not have enough time to go there and back. Finally, I asked if they would accept Thai baht, and luckily, they did. As I went through customs, something in my backpack triggered the alarms. I was called back and told to empty my bag. The guy kept touching the bottom of my pack, saying 'bullet', I didn't understand. Eventually, after presenting my spare cane and a padlock and chain that I never used, the guy found the object in question at the bottom of my pack. It was a wooden plaque I had purchased in Australia; it contained a piece of metal and had alarmed the sensors. Once that was resolved, I was allowed through.

A member of the Vietnamese airport staff took me to wait for my flight and then just as I was settling down, something was announced in Vietnamese and everybody disappeared and I was left sitting there alone. I realised that the gate number had been changed and I waved my arms to get some attention until eventually an airport official took me to the correct gate. I finally left Vietnam. One hour later I arrived in Bangkok and the last part of my magnificent trip began.

Bangkok

Bangkok is the most incredible city I have ever visited. That drive from the airport into the city takes an age. Once out of the airport, having been assisted by the friendly staff – they all seemed to smile in Thailand – I took a taxi to the HI in the heart of the city. It took nearly two hours to get there. The heat was intense and the traffic fumes were overpowering. It was as bad as Los Angeles, if not worse. The hostel was in a small street, not too far from the famous Kao San Road. I went up a large concrete step and entered an open house. Unfortunately, I stepped in without removing my footwear and was shouted at because it's a Buddhist custom to remove shoes before entering. I said I had a reservation for five nights, and a small lady showed me up some steep narrow stairs to a crowded dorm. I claimed a bed next to the fan, which barely worked. The place was stifling and water dripped everywhere. The bathroom was horrible. Some people would not have stomached such surroundings, but I was used to simple requirements. I hadn't been brushing my teeth since I had left for SEA and used bottled water when I was not drinking alcohol.

It was early evening when I arrived and I found a restaurant at the front of the hostel. I met a Dutch traveller named Mark, and a couple of English girls who were on the last part of their world trip. My main reason for visiting Thailand was to go to the bridge over the River Kwai, part of the famous WWII story. A Prisoner of War camp had been established there and the Japanese had set the captives to work to build a bridge to connect Burma with Thailand and the remainder of Asia. The British planned a coercive operation to destroy the bridge and mostly succeeded. The two English girls had just been to the bridge on a two-day excursion. They asked me who I was travelling with and when I said I was alone they were amazed and offered to help me organise a trip to the bridge. We rode in a tuk-tuk, a three-wheel, colourful taxi to the Kao San Road and then walked. You have to be aware of the drivers as they try to charge an excessive amount. The atmosphere was incredible; there were several backpacker accommodations along that stretch as it was Bangkok's main tourist road. There were people selling all kinds of items from burnt CDs from the Internet to t-shirts, books and tours of all descriptions.

Eventually, we found the travel shop that offered excursions. One of the girls, named Lisa, asked about a tour to the bridge for me. She read out what the excursion involved, and I could do a day trip or longer. I debated doing the two day excursion as that included an elephant ride, but I was unsure about cancelling my accommodation in Bangkok, which I had already booked. I later realised I could have gone, but that's life!

After booking the one-day tour, the girls and I had a drink in a roadside café and swapped travel stories. We returned to the hostel as the girls had a flight to catch and it was damned hot. Mark and I later went to the nearby 7/11 store to buy some food and beer.

I met some other backpackers from England, a guy from Liverpool and his girlfriend. I was in the lounge when they arrived. This was an expansive area with a reception in one corner and scattered seating. There was a large fridge where beer was stored and several small tables by the entrance where a couple of young female Thai students sat each evening. They came to learn English and help the guests. I made a joke when I heard that the English guy was from Liverpool and we got chatting immediately. I also met another English couple who were even friendlier and we hung around together for several days. The guy from Liverpool asked me how long I had been travelling and who with, and when I told him I was 'solo', he was astonished. I explained that I just wanted to explore and travel, and I used the public to help get around.

Towards the end of that trip, recognition and self-awareness began to dawn; I was beginning to realise that my blindness was not a burden, which stopped me from accomplishing things, but an attribute, which opened more doors than it closed. I recognised it was all about mental attitude. The positive responses I gained from fellow travellers highlighted to me that it was my character, not my blindness that was more noticeable.

There were five or six of us who hung around together for most of the week. Two other English girls arrived one evening, but I dismissed them as moaning tourists after half an hour in their company. One hilarity occurred while I was quietly relaxing in the lounge, a girl screamed and jumped high into the air.

"It's a cockroach." I said, laughing. "He's harmless."

The roach wasn't our only visitor. One night, a large black rodent about 8 inches (20 centimetres) tall came and sat by the fridge. Someone said, "Tony, there's Ratty. Go open the fridge for him, he's hungry!"

I said, "He's not having my bloody beer!"

Mark and I spent an afternoon exploring some of the city. We visited temples, one of which had a reclining Buddha. We walked around the massive open area and removed our sandals before entering the temple. The Buddha was made from marble and lay on a long table; I was able to touch his feet. He was huge! At his head, there was a large gong. Mark put his head inside it and I gave it a bang. The air was heavy with incense. Mark told me that people were being offered Thai massages; I smiled, denoting the double entendre. We went to the Grand Palace but decided it was too expensive to visit.

I was able to touch several statues in another smaller temple garden, including several stone lions. We walked to the Chao Praya River and took a boat down stream like in the James Bond film, *Man with the Golden Gun* (1974). The open, crowded boat hardly stopped and you are meant to jump on and off. Thankfully, one did stop for us and I was helped off at the other end, before the boat moved again. We then took a bus; I sat in the front seat and was promptly admonished for sitting in a seat reserved for the monks. Once in the centre, we boarded a sky train that traversed the central area. Mark needed to get to the Cambodian Embassy before 5 pm to collect his visa, which would allow him to cross into Cambodia from Thailand, and then venture into Laos if the border was open.

We eventually found the correct embassy and Mark waited for around twenty minutes for his documents before we made our way slowly back across the city to the hostel. Once again, I was confronted by an area that would have been nearly impossible to explore alone. The hectic traffic hardly ever stopped for anyone, although it did heed to traffic signals, unlike in Vietnam. There were large holes and drainage ditches everywhere, not to mention broken bridges and open gaps in the pavements. It would have taken all my skills and concentration to try going alone.

During our return journey, Mark, who would try any food, stopped and bought some pancakes with cherries in. We tried a fruit that resembled a small banana but contained hard seeds. I liked this one because it was sweet. The pancakes were delicious, containing either chicken or fruit. We also saw fried cockroach for sale on an open market, but even Mark refused that!

I found it fascinating walking around observing the culture with my other senses. Was this why I was meant to be blind – to absorb what so many other people miss, the real sensations of life?

I spent that evening drinking and socialising. The next day I was collected from the hostel soon after 7 am by a guy in a small car and driven to meet a bus to go to the River Kwai. Several more people were collected before we took a long drive into the country. I got talking with some of the group, particularly with a girl from New Zealand named Laura. Our first stop was Kenchanaburi War Cemetery, which contained 6,982 graves. They were divided into rows of British, Thai and other nationalities. I walked around, trying not to step on any of the graves, and found Laura who was hunting for New Zealand burials. We found several and she could not get over the age of them.

"So young," she said.

I told her all I knew about the area, the bridge and the significance to the war. She could tell that I was an enthusiast.

While we were waiting for the remainder of the group, Laura showed me a tactile map of the area. I could not believe it. Here I was, in the middle of the Thailand bush, and there was a tactile map with the river and all the major prison camps marked, just in case a blind person came along! What a treat and a nice surprise.

Next, we went to find the bridge and the museum, where we were given an hour to explore. Laura and

I visited the museum but we were so busy talking that we never found the bridge, even though we were so near to it. It was just a small construction, which had been rebuilt after its sabotage. The museum had many pictures of the camp and the prisoners in different states of emaciation. There were also a few guns and a bomb or two that I was able to touch.

After stopping at the bridge, we had lunch in a clearing. The group and I separated and I took a train ride. I was driven down to the old track where I boarded a small steam train. The track paralleled the river on a really narrow cliff, which eventually became quite steep. I smelt the smoke and felt the train's every jolt. The trip took about an hour. The guide met me at the other end and we began the long journey back to Bangkok, stopping along the way for refreshments. The sun was really penetrating and once we left the smog of Bangkok, it was bright and strong.

I arrived back in Bangkok around 7 pm. It had been an interesting tour, although I was sorry not to have walked the bridge. But that's the nature of travelling.

One evening I was a spectator at some kickboxing, the national sport of Thailand. We sat on large concrete steps and witnessed about fifteen bouts of semi-professional boxing and, to finish, one match of orthodox boxing. The stadium was big and quite empty with little atmosphere but the fights were good. They lasted three or six rounds each, though the last fight was over in less than thirty seconds. The two boxers entered, bowed, as is the Asian custom, and then one guy hit the other, knocked him out and we all left. As we ventured back to the hostel, we passed through what seemed to be a market or fair, where I attempted to hit a dartboard. One of the girls said, "I didn't know you played darts, Tony?"

I said, "I have many hidden talents, my dear!" They all had a good laugh at my efforts.

Ross and I, who have since become good friends, met during the last two days of my trip. I was relaxing when I heard this American voice.

We began a conversation and quickly became companions. He was a tall, strong twenty-two year old and was travelling the world. We shared a taxi to the airport where we had a long wait for our flights. Mark left, along with many of the others, although he went north while the others went south to the beaches and islands. I could have gone with any of them and extended my stay in Thailand, but by then I had been travelling for long enough. I was ready to stop running – until the next time.

Epilogue

I feel that I'm the luckiest person alive for being able to undertake these journeys. I was given chances, which I took, to make everything possible and eventually created my own opportunities.

The US, first time around, was enchanting and fantastic. The South was charming and unique. My education gave me a view of the world and a chance to escape. Once my journey had begun, there was no looking back. The security of university enabled me to gain confidence, to fear nothing and try everything, as this book has illustrated. South Carolina and New Orleans were the catalyst, and Australia and New Zealand were an extension of that desire to explore and enact my own dreams, find excitement and escapism, with no restrictions or barriers.

My US trips had been a revelation and mainly enjoyable. I had met people from all backgrounds and society and it had helped my studies immensely. The best way to research a country's history and culture is to investigate it in the nation you are studying. I had that opportunity, and by making friends was able to observe the US at close quarters. I took advantage of every situation available, which enabled me to visit New Orleans, California, and Hawaii, if only briefly.

Southern and Central Australia was fascinating, with

its history, unique culture, cities and desert. The coasts were electrifying, particularly the east coast with its activities and wildlife and the west coast with its barren expanses. One day, I'll return to Perth, explore more of the west and east coasts, enter the desert, visit Broom and go north beyond Cairns.

New Zealand was fantastic and is, to date, my favourite country visited. North Island was delightful, the people were friendly and the activities I did were tremendous. Rotorua was the highlight and the bungee jump in Taihape was the best activity. However, this was nothing compared to South Island with its enormity of diverse wilderness. The scenery of the west coast alone was enough to leave me breathless, not to mention the plethora of activities, nature walks, hikes and adrenalin events to suit all.

New Zealand has everything, from lakes and glaciers to lush vegetation and full flowing rivers. However, its people, more than anything, are superb. Their relaxed and generous nature, their attitude towards me, added to my admiration for the country. I hope to return eventually and backpack without a bus tour to help me around, which made the trip quite comfortable and easy. Travelling New Zealand the alternative way is my future challenge!

What little of South East Asia I visited more than surpassed any expectation. Vietnam was wonderful; the food was amazing and the people were friendly, knowledgeable and very kind. They were inquisitive, polite, hard working and enchanting. I would recommend a visit to anyone. The war history is fascinating, but for people less inclined, there is wonderful culture, environment and many other enticements to suit all. Vietnam has opened up even more since I was there and I would love to return and explore the entire country – another journey for the future. Thailand incidentally was fantastic. Bangkok is still the most amazing city I've visited; it vibrates with activity and atmosphere. Although I experienced little of the country, what I did witness was enough to make me want to return for a longer visit. The spicy food aside, everything else is to my liking. An inexpensive and fascinating country for any backpacker with an ounce of passion for culture and adventure.

Landing in London around 10th March 2002 and heading back to Weston-super-Mare to visit my family closed this first chapter of my global travels.

Where Are They Now?

You may be wondering what has happened to some of the people I met during these travels.

My Australian friend Kate O'Brien, the girl I met and travelled with in the US and later went to visit in Melbourne, is doing fine. She worked and travelled in the UK for two years and stayed with me when I rented my first flat in 2005. She's now returned to Australia and we are in regular contact.

Will Harris, my disabled school friend and fellow traveller, is still around. We talk and meet up frequently. We continue to hostel and go to concerts together and our shared love of live music continues.

Marcia is doing as well as can be expected in South Carolina. Ross, the guy I met in Thailand keeps busy, and has spent time studying in New Zealand – lucky man.

The guys I met in New Zealand – the two Pauls, Deanna, Cane and the other travellers have all disappeared, except for the young lady I slept with on that memorable summer's night. She remains anonymous, but she's doing ok. The other people I met in Australia and in South East Asia are sadly no longer in contact with me.

I'm still in touch with Geoff, my mature friend from Coastal Carolina University and also Jimmy G, the one surviving member of the gang from that time. Geoff is still working at the university and Jimmy G has a job in the publishing world and lives in London.

It is great to have travel contacts and friends to reminisce with about good times and great travels – until we do it all again!

If you've enjoyed this book and you want to know more about Tony and his global adventures please visit his website:

www.tonythetraveller.com

Bibliography

Amor, D, *Guide to the Political Map of Australasia*
(London, The Royal National Institute for the Blind, 1983)

Green, Graham, *The Quiet American*
(London, William Heinemann, 1955)

Karnow, Stanley, *Vietnam: A History*
(USA; Viking Press, 1983)

Kolko, Gabriel, *Anatomy of a Peace*
(London; Routledge, 1997)

Kolko, Gabriel, *Anatomy of a War*
(New York; New Press, 1985)

Miller, Arthur, *The Crucible*
(New York; Viking Press 1953)

Ngor, Haing Dr. A., *Cambodian Odyssey*
(London; Chatto and Windus Ltd., 1988)

Ryon, James, et al, *Lonely Planet USA*
(Melbourne; Lonely Planet Publishing, 1999)

Lightning Source UK Ltd.
Milton Keynes UK

177716UK00001B/55/P